THE
RIPPLE
EFFECT

SUE JORGENSEN

RIVERHEAD

Sue Jorgensen

A CIP catalogue record for this book is
available from the British Library

ISBN 978-1-9164294-3-7

Design and Production by Riverhead
Kardomah 94,
94 Alfred Gelder Street, Hull HU1 2AN
Telephone: 07890 170063
email: mike.riverheadbooks@gmail.com

Printed by: Fisk Printers, Hull

CONTENTS

Sue Jorgensen

THE RIPPLE EFFECT

The best way I can describe 'the ripple effect' is that Michael was like a stone that was thrown into a pond. The water rippled out and I was there to stop the first ripple, so nothing passed me and I took the full brunt of Michael's PTSD.

Sue Jorgensen

This is a true story that recalls the traumatic events of one sunny Sunday afternoon and how they affected our lives during the following five years…

CHAPTER 1
THE ACCIDENT

In May 2014, just over five years ago, I was a happily married, forty-seven year old woman, with two amazing children, a girl aged 17 and a boy aged 25.

I worked part-time as a personal assistant for a lovely lady, Janet and also for an adorable little boy, named Kian.

It was a lovely sunny Sunday morning, I was getting ready for work as although I had a bad headache, I knew I had to go to Janet's house to help her get dressed for the day.

The morning was running smoothly but my headache was getting worse and I couldn't wait for 2 o'clock to go home as I wanted to go to bed for an hour to try and get rid of the headache. I decided to leave my phone downstairs so I didn't get disturbed.

Not long after I laid down my mobile started ringing but I ignored it. Then the house line started ringing and I just laid there thinking, God, I've got a really bad headache, they'll have to wait.

Over the years since that terrible Sunday afternoon I have often thought that I wasn't meant to answer that phonecall. I never normally went back to bed. It was fate watching out for me. If I'd answered the phone I would have gone looking for Michael and probably caused, or had an accident myself. But both phones kept ringing and I thought it must be important because they weren't stopping.

I went downstairs and the answer-phone was flashing, so I pressed play and heard my poor son crying and screaming out for me to help him. But the only words I could understand were, "I've killed him."

He was shouting, "Help mam, help! I've killed someone, help me mam, help me!"

I quickly grabbed my mobile phone and rang him but there was no answer. I rang his girlfriend, Kate, but she didn't know anything about what had happened. So I tried ringing him again but there was still no answer.

My heart was racing.

I thought I was going crazy. I needed to know what was wrong with my son. Then the house phone rang again. It was the ambulance services saying someone had been killed and my son was in shock.

I remember shouting, "Was it my son's fault?" and they said "No."

I cried out, "Where are you? I'm coming," and they told me to make my way to Hull Royal Infirmary.

As I put the phone down, Kate appeared at the door with her mum wanting to know what was happening. I explained as best I could with the tears running down my face.

Then my son's employers, Asda Kingswood, rang me to let me know that they were aware there had been an accident and they were unsure as to how to approach the question but asked me what state the delivery van was in. I told them I believed it was a write off and they thanked me, sending their regards and saying they would be in touch.

Then we both made our way to see Michael at the hospital. The nurses told us we had to wait but I couldn't just stand there so I looked behind all the curtains until I found him. He looked up at me and started sobbing in my arms. The doctor at the hospital told me he was still in shock and bruised but they allowed him to go home but said we needed to keep an eye on him. We took him to his flat as he didn't want to go back to my house.

He didn't talk on the way, he just cried but when we got to his flat he started telling me what had happened.

As he sobbed, he explained that he'd been driving his Asda van, taking a delivery to Bridlington.

He'd been driving on a country road, he got to a blind bend when a sports car passed him on the opposite side of the road and he thought, what a fucking prick!

Then, as he carried on round the corner a motorbike was on his side of the road and he swerved but the bike also swerved to miss the van, which created a head on crash.

Michael said it was like slow motion and that the motorcyclist was so close that he could see into his eyes and the stubble on his face.

He parked his van the best he could and he ran to the lad as his legs were kicking. As he approached him he was shouting and asking if he was okay and he said he would get help. But when he reached him he realised that he had been decapitated.

He turned round back to the van to get the work phone to be confronted by the sight of the front and side of the van covered in blood. He then went into shock.

By this time, a number of cars had stopped and a lovely couple took my son, sat him down and looked after him until the ambulance arrived.

He stayed up and cried most of the night; I stayed with him together with his girlfriend. The police removed his mobile phone at the scene. My husband looked after my daughter and my three foster children.

The next day the police came to take a statement as it all had to be investigated and they had to do it as soon as possible so it was fresh in everyone's minds. Michael sobbed as he explained again what had happened and the police told us that the lad in the sports car, who was the biker's best friend, had been arrested.

Witnesses had come forward to say that the biker, a lad called Owen, and the driver of the sports car had been racing each other.

After the police left, the manager from Asda turned up and said they would help in any way they could and that Michael shouldn't worry about his job, which I thought was nice of them.

I took Michael to the doctor as the hospital had suggested. The doctor thought he had a couple of cracked ribs and gave him some painkillers and something to calm him down.

That's when the devil, PTSD took control.

Whenever Michael closed his eyes all that he saw was Owen's face. Then the panic attacks and anxiety started and the triggers made it difficult for him to fall asleep as the accident played over and over in his mind.

He started self-harming and drinking, as Owen would speak to him in his dreams, asking him why he'd killed him, causing a sleep disorder.

THE RIPPLE EFFECT

We were told he had to go to the inquest but asked the doctor if there was any way that Michael could get out of this as it would be too stressful and the thought of it was already making his anxiety much worse. He said that Michael must go and to help he should take the tablets he'd prescribed.

At the inquest we found out the two lads were on army leave and that the police were not going to press charges on the lad in the car as, 'He had to live with the death of his best friend.'

Also they did not speed through the town but there were lots of witnesses to say they were speeding on the country roads.

I spoke to Owen's mum in the toilet and she told me how worried she was about Owen's friend, and about how he was going to cope.

Inside I was screaming, 'What about Michael?'

I think it was logged as 'accidental death' as the motorbike was too big for him to handle. Owen died that day and so did my son. I won't tell you any more about the accident, as it was really horrible. When the police returned Michael's phone, they took me to one side and said that it was the worst accident they'd ever attended and because of what Michael had seen he would need lots of help.

The anger that I felt towards Owen and his friend was unbelievable. It started eating me up like a cancer. Their stupidity had left my son 'dead behind the eyes and with a tortured mind'.

He had two years of counselling and therapy but he would carry the Post Traumatic Stress Disorder forever.

What do you do when your son feels worthless?

He turned to drink and drugs, nearly lost his flat and his job and I was trying to keep it together for him.

In the summer of 2014, Asda sorted some therapy out for Michael and I took him to five sessions. But the lady was taken poorly and I think she passed away so it ended suddenly and it was the solicitor who sorted out the other counsellors.

Michael had not had any compensation yet so that was why his dad and I were paying for everything.

This was when Owen's mum could have helped as he could have lost his house. That was when Michael said the Manager didn't like him and I tend to agree with this.

As for the army, they didn't give a shit. Why didn't they ask if they could help? Surely they could have put him in group therapy with their people.

After six months, Michael returned to work at Asda as a 'floater'. He couldn't drive the van because of the triggers, so he worked on the tills or did general duties such as collecting the trollies. But he didn't get paid if he didn't go to work.

Michael could have good days and go to work, but then this might bring on an attack or a trigger that meant when he arrived at work he couldn't even get out of the car...

The first manager of Asda left and he got a new manager who was fantastic, as she understood Post Traumatic Stress Disorder. She has been his rock and he sings her praises all the time. When he had an attack she brought him round. She was a truly amazing woman...

There were times when Michael wouldn't turn up for work after night terrors and he would lock himself away for days. I turned up at his flat one day and the smell coming from it was terrible. I let myself in and he was sitting on the sofa with his dressing gown hood covering his face. He had not slept for days. There was sewage all over the place as there had been a blockage in the street. The overflow had been running all over the bathroom and hallway and his flat had been like that for a day and a half. The bath was full of sewage and he told me he wanted to leave it like that, as that is what he deserved, as he was worthless. He didn't want me to clean it up or ring 'housing' as he wanted to live like that.

The doctor kept trying him on different medication to find one to suit him especially when his PTSD was bad. When I tried to talk to him I'd get upset. He talked of going to group therapy, as people there talked about how they coped when they had killed someone.

I tried everything. I contacted Brake, Scarred, Mind, Talk, and the Mental Health Team but no one seemed able to help. They all needed to talk to him but they didn't have the training for this type of thing. They only did 'one to one' and he didn't want that. He wanted to do a group session as he had already done two years of 'one to one'.

I had to try to protect my husband and daughter from this as when my daughter had witnessed Michael having a panic attack, it broke her heart and really scared her.

I cried in private, as I didn't want the ripple effect to spread beyond me and effect other members of my family. I was broken along with Michael and I kept hitting brick walls...

CHAPTER 2
WHY COULDN'T I FORGIVE THEM?

By the time Michael had returned to work Asda had another Manager but Michael told me he didn't think the new Manager liked him. I asked Michael why? and he explained it was because the Manager didn't seem to have any time for him and always tried to avoid him whenever he could.

I told Michael not to worry and that he'd be fine. Sometime later he had a really bad attack at work and was sent home. He was crying and said again that the new Manager didn't like him so I decided to ask for a meeting with the Manager behind Michael's back. They arranged one for 8.30 the next morning.

I didn't tell Michael and the following day made my way to Asda to see the People's Manager and the Store Manager. I explained that Michael's PTSD was severe and he had lots of triggers but he tried his best and if he didn't turn up it was because he'd possibly had night terrors and had stayed awake for days as he was scared to go to sleep.

He didn't ring the Mental Health team because he didn't want to talk about it, as that only made it worse.

He didn't always take my calls and on more than one occasion I had to send his dad to the flat to make sure he hadn't taken his own life.

THE RIPPLE EFFECT

The new Store Manager lounged on a two-seater sofa with his legs up, drinking a coffee. He said when Michael had an attack it took two members of staff off the shop floor and that they were a business and it had been two years now since the accident.

I said he couldn't help the PTSD and it did happen at work and it didn't help that Owen's mum kept putting things in the local paper and when Michael saw the face that he sees in his dreams it brought on an attack.

The Store Manager replied that maybe that was how she was grieving and perhaps they needed to cut Michael's hours. I disagreed and said he still had to pay his bills and life needed to be as normal as possible. I left with all this going round in my head and how I hated Owen and his best friend for leaving my son with a tortured life and I couldn't help thinking how the Manager didn't give a damn and that he couldn't understand the trauma of PTSD.

I decided to write to the Managing Director of Asda and the following week his secretary rang me to say they'd received my letter and were aware of the accident.

I told her the full graphic details. Everything. The kind of things that nightmares are made of. Things that Michael now saw every day.

Even Owen's mum didn't know the full details of his injuries, as they were thought to be too horrific and the police felt that it was better for some things to be left unsaid. But I told the poor woman on the phone everything and she promised me that she would pass it on to the MD.

Surprise, surprise, Asda rang a few days later and I

was asked to go back. This time there was only the People's Manager there. I asked where the Store Manager was and she said that he was busy. I sat down and she went on to say that Michael's job would always be safe and they would not be cutting his hours. I asked again where the Store Manager was and again her reply was that he was busy. I've never spoken to him since, so maybe Michael was right...

The psychiatrist and therapist had been by his side. But I didn't say much about this to my husband and daughter, as I didn't want the ripple effect to affect them.

I knew how the anger and hatred was inside me.

Owen got off lightly. He was dead. But Michael was tortured every day. I believe in God and forgiveness so why couldn't I forgive them for 'destroying' my son?

I wrote to 'This Morning' to see if they could help Michael with his panic attacks and his triggers. They did reply and said it was too severe and gave me some numbers to ring but I had already tried all those.

I even tried contacting Russell Brand as I knew he had fought his own demons. I tried for weeks but couldn't find him. My thoughts were, Please, please help me to find someone to help Michael.

I couldn't tell anyone as I didn't want the ripple effect to affect my husband, daughter and the other children. There was no point in anyone else suffering these dark times.

My anger continued to be vented towards Owen's mum and dad as well.

Understanding the loss of a child is unthinkable but

in my mind Owen and his friend's stupidity had made my son tortured, so I couldn't feel anything for any of them. And now I kick myself. I should have shouted, "My son's done nothing wrong. Now he has a mental illness! You crazy woman, worrying about his friend."

And although they insisted Michael wasn't in any way to blame for Owen's death, neither did they admit that Owen had been driving dangerously and speeding on the afternoon of the accident. I felt that these facts should have been made clear in the court as they were major factors in a lot of Michael's problems and his feeling of guilt.

I watched my son being tortured daily. He was the innocent party and my anger grew towards Owen's mum and dad and his friend who had been driving the car.

They did a charity event in memory of Owen and put his face in our local paper. Michael saw that face every time he closed his eyes, and there it was in the paper for him to see again. After Michael saw the photo, Owen again asked Michael in his dreams why he had killed him?

It put Michael back again. One step forward, two steps back…

Later that year, in November 2014, Owen's mum wrote a book titled 'Smile' about the accident and the loss of her son, and again an article about it appeared in the local paper. That was when I decided to write to her. My husband disagreed but I did it because as far as I was concerned it kept putting Michael backwards. I kindly asked her to stop putting things in the local paper as she was 'messing with my son's head'. She never replied but I'm pleased to say things stopped going in the local paper.

I was having difficulty forgiving, I prayed for guidance but I couldn't do it because I hated Owen. And I felt that because I hated Owen I couldn't let his soul move on. This wasn't me but once Michael was better I would let Owen's soul go. I hated myself for not finding forgiveness in my heart.

I felt like a headless chicken with all these thoughts, keeping it together for my son and hiding my sadness to protect my husband, daughter and the other children from the ripple effect.

As the anger grew in me my husband noticed the changes in me. Every second of every day I was thinking about Michael, asking what I could do to make things better? His dad and I were paying his bills and I cleaned his flat and made sure that he was clean and had plenty of food.

Everything had changed on Sunday May 25th 2014.

Michael had lost all his friends, and he'd hide away, hating himself and thinking that he was worthless. It was heartbreaking to watch. Every day I never knew if I was going to find his body. He had promised me not to take his own life but the psychiatrist found that he had been cutting and burning himself and putting pins down his nails to feel anything other than guilt.

Christmas was a very bad time for him as he'd learnt that Owen was an only child and Michael cried with guilt that Owen's mum would never have anyone or have grandchildren but I told him that was not his fault. I repeatedly told him he'd done nothing wrong and that Owen had killed himself.

The thought - God, I hate that family - went through my head again and again. But I then put a smile on my face and tried my best to protect my family from the darkness that I felt inside.

My daughter Sharma's birthday was coming up. I would have a party, not too many people, and we would paint a smile on our faces even though we were both dying inside.

Michael's cousins came and I noticed that one of them had been a bit funny towards Michael's girlfriend. I let it pass. Michael's girlfriend Kate was going away with her mum and a friend but said Michael could go with them so we paid for him to go, hoping it would do him some good. I bumped into my nephew and asked why some of the cousins had been off with Kate and I was told it was because she had slept with one of his cousins. I rang the cousin and asked him to meet me, and then I asked him if it was true? He denied it at first but then he admitted it. I told him I had to tell Michael as everyone else knew except us.

A couple of days later when I was alone with Michael at his flat, I told him. He guessed straight away who it was. He had already had his suspicions and had actually asked him. The relationship ended after five years.

I still talked to Kate as she was supporting Michael at the worst time of his life. But then once again things spiralled out of control tenfold.

The nightmares and the flashbacks got worse. I sometimes wished that I hadn't said anything, even though I knew it would only have been a matter of time before he'd found out.

I rang the mental health team crying and not knowing what I was going to do with Michael. They said he had to ring them himself but I knew that wouldn't happen…

A little later, I realised that I had started to break away from my own siblings. I'm one of six, and I always thought that we were a close family. Now I realised that we were not.

The lads often had parties at the weekend, but not once did they ask Michael or me to go. Not one of them cared what was going on, they didn't reach out to him. Not one of them cared about the hell he was going through. It was like Michael meant nothing to them. At least that was the way I felt. My whole childhood had been a lie! Not one of them held out a branch to my son. No one cared. Even Michael asked why he wasn't invited? What could I say? That no one cared?

Michael's Great Auntie Sue and her son Nick and daughter Faye were the only ones that turned up at his flat and invited him to go to theirs. My family had kind of lost me as their sister. When I needed them most, no one looked out for my son and me.

When my husband Gerald asked me how things were, I played it down; making out that everything was okay. My daughter Sharma was training to be a nurse. I didn't want her to be stressed, so I stopped the ripple effect passing from me...

CHAPTER 3
THE DARKEST DAYS

At the beginning of 2015 I started going to a counselling meeting every Thursday and it really helped me. My counsellor, Keith, thought that I had Secondary Trauma Syndrome caused by Michael's trauma. I looked it up and I agreed with him.

I kept telling them at the meetings that I needed to find forgiveness so that Owen's soul could move on and I prayed for guidance again. I think this time He was listening because fate started to take control.

I did a lot of ranting and raving at Keith, who sat there listening to me going on and on, but not saying much until I asked, "Well, what would you do then?" and "What should I do?"

We even laughed together although I'm sure that he thought I was off my rocker.

As for my husband, he didn't say much either. And I didn't really tell him much as I didn't want him to suffer from the ripple effect...

Later that week Michael received a letter from the court for £500 Council Tax and he hadn't earned enough as it had gone up so his dad and me paid it. A week later he got another letter saying he owed £520 in rent, so we arranged to pay it monthly.

Michael was still very up and down but he also gave me faith. One day I was with him and I asked how he would feel if I got a solicitor, as I still felt Owen's best friend had got away with dangerous driving. I was told that he'd been on leave from the army and that he would have to live with Owen's death for the rest of his life. But there were a number of witnesses that saw him racing with Owen, so why wasn't he charged with something?

Again I couldn't help but think that if some blame had been attached to Owen and his friend for the accident, then it may have helped Michael to realise that he wasn't to blame!

To my surprise Michael hugged me and said, "No mam, how do you know he's not like me, fucked in the head? He may be fighting his own demons."

Wow! What a wonderful, kind thing, it was, not to have hate in his heart, I thought.

I took a deep breath and said, "Do you forgive Owen for making you ill?"

"Yes, of course I do," he replied.

"He wouldn't have gone out that day thinking, right, I'm going to go out and destroy someone's life, then kill myself. And he paid the ultimate price, he died."

That put my brain into overdrive. How could he be so forgiving when I couldn't? And to make things worse I wouldn't let Owen's soul move on until Michael was better. So I decided to read Owen's mum's book to find out what he had been like and maybe find a way to forgive him.

I remember another day during the very dark times, when things were very different. I was at Michael's flat.

THE RIPPLE EFFECT

He hadn't been to sleep for days and the sleeping tablets made him dysfunctional the next day and he always hid his face with the dressing gown hood so that I couldn't see his tears. He wouldn't let me stay, and asked me to leave as he didn't want to see anyone, so I did as he asked.

I sat in my car and cried and rang the mental health team again who were understanding but couldn't help unless he rang himself. But that wasn't going to happen. He'd had two years of counselling. I kept sending him a text asking if he was all right and asking him to reply with a 'Yes' or an 'X' so I would know he was okay. After a couple of hours I'd still not had a reply, so I then sent a begging text, "Please Michael, send me something so I know you're okay."

Nothing!

My eyes filled up and my heart was racing. I didn't want to go to his flat and find his body so I begged him to send me a text so I would know he was alive. But still there was no reply!

I sent my husband, and that is the most scared I had been and it seemed forever before he rang to tell me that Michael was in a state and had smashed his phone.

His dad stayed with him for a while and they talked but then a thought ran through my head – that everybody shut the door on me and nobody was making him well.

I decided that I was going to tie myself to the Humber Bridge! Not to threaten to kill myself but to say I wouldn't come down until someone looked after my boy. I thought about that a few times.

They would think I was committing suicide but I

wasn't. But then the rational side of my mind would kick in and say, yes they would agree to everything but then I would be tied up and stuck in 'the nut house' and they would forget about my son and I would be back to square one.

I saw on the TV that Prince William and Prince Harry wanted more help for people with mental health problems and post stress disorder. I thought yes, yes if it was them they would be put in The Priory until they were cured. In fact only the wealthy get the help but us minions get what we can from the National Health.

Then I thought about contacting Russell Brand again, as he was beating his demons and I'm sure he would have helped. If he does read my story one day, perhaps he will contact me.

One day out of the blue he thought Bear Grylls could help him deal with his demons, my daughter contacted the show but we didn't hear anything. We would try anything to help Michael. I kept the anger to myself as I didn't want to create the ripple effect.

My wonderful daughter Sharma, had helped whenever she could. She met a lovely Scottish lad when she was training in Scotland to be a disability nurse. I was happy for her to go but missed her loads. But she didn't need all the hell and the worry. A clear mind and soul was what I wanted for her.

A few weeks later, it was in the paper that Owen's mum was doing a charity event, and that the profit from the book was going to the 'Help for Heroes' charity.

I couldn't help but think, why hasn't she contacted me and asked if there was anything she could do for me, like help to send Michael to The Priory or pay his bills or rent?

A few times during the following weeks it even crossed my mind to go and see Owen's mum and dad to scream at them, "Please help me make my son well."

Due to his mental state things were not getting paid and we were paying Michael's bills as well as our own. I wanted him to move back home but couldn't do that because of my foster children. He didn't want to lose his home, he had already lost his mind. She could at least have asked. And as for the army, who were at court, why didn't they take me to one side to ask if there was anything they could do?

I would have said, 'Yes, put him in the support groups for PTSD."

But nobody gave a damn. We didn't get any help from anyone. He was an army lad, so why didn't they realise the hell that we would have to face?

I felt that when we walked out of the court it was done and dusted for them but my nightmare was just beginning…

I know it sounds mad but I'd try anything to help Michael and once again the thought of tying myself to the Humber Bridge crossed my mind. But people would think I was going to commit suicide when I was really saying, "I will not come down unless someone looks after my son and makes him well."

Then one day on Facebook I saw a soldier from the USA, saying how he'd written a story on PTSD and how he'd helped himself to get better. I even messaged him to see if he could help me but I didn't get a reply. So again I tried Mind, Break, Scarred, Talk, Mental

Health, This Morning, Russell Brand and Bear Grylls, but no one could help and no one ran PTSD groups that Michael wanted to attend. He didn't want anymore 'one to ones'.

In October 2015, nearly a year and a half after the accident, I got three beautiful and amazing foster children to keep me busy but everything was hidden from them like it had been from my husband and daughter. There were still two of me - the one at home, happy and smiling - and the other one with Michael, screaming inside...

CHAPTER 4
THE STRANGER IN THE PARK

One day in the Spring of 2016 Michael was in a very dark place and he wanted me out of his flat. His eyes were black, he was punching himself in the face and he asked me to leave. I left with tears in my eyes and went to sit in my car wondering what I could do.

I decided to walk the dog as I live next to a beautiful big park and this helped me to clear my mind. So I got my dog and took her for a walk. It was a lovely day and as soon as I got to the park I let her off her lead.

I texted Michael to tell him that I was there for him. As I walked around the park, my heart was aching, and my eyes filled with tears and I started to cry.

A man of a similar age to me stopped me in my tracks and asked if I was okay. You know what it's like when someone asks you if you're okay. Asking me that question had made me begin to sob again. I started to tell the stranger about Michael and the disease and how every time I tried to get help, nobody was there for us and all I got was the same response that he had to ring them himself.

The man just listened to me and said, 'I don't tell everyone this but I also have PTSD. Eight years have passed and I'm just starting to see the light at the end of the tunnel.'

He told me that his mum and brother had died in a fire and he was the only survivor.

'This will be with me for the rest of my life,' he explained. 'But I will learn to live with it and things will get better. It does take time but carry on with what you're doing,' he advised.

After the fire he thought his life would never be the same and he would never be happy like he had been again but now his life was slowly changing for the better.

'So don't give up hope,' he told me.

We walked around the park together. He was a complete stranger but I had never felt so close to someone. I thanked him and we parted and I've never seen the man again.

After this conversation I knew it was going to be a long road to recovery. But if he could see the light at the end of the tunnel, maybe there was hope for Michael.

A few days later I had another strange experience! Michael was in a state and when he was in a state, so was I. It was strange, but my moods mirrored his.

It was another lovely, warm day but I knew Michael was in a bad place again. I thought I would walk my dog down a remote track and it would give me the perfect opportunity to clear my thoughts.

I decided to call out to God, 'Why isn't anyone helping to save my son? Please God, help me!' I begged, as tears rolled down my face. I needed someone to save my boy from his living hell.

If the devil had said to me, 'Give me your soul and Michael will be fine,' he wouldn't have had to ask twice because my children are my life.

THE RIPPLE EFFECT

As I walked with all these thoughts going through my head, my phone suddenly pinged. I opened it and I couldn't believe what I saw. It was a notification of a friend's celebration with the song playing 'You get by with a little help from your friends'.

The notification was full of photos and memories with them. I couldn't believe it. It made me smile and I thought someone was listening to me. It was really perfect timing for me.

What I was trying to clarify is that when PTSD is talked about, everyone seemed to think that it was just people who have been in the Army who suffer with it. What they didn't seem to realise was that it can happen to anyone, at any age, anywhere.

I even contacted the Lee Rigby Foundation and told them about my struggles with PTSD. They were amazing and replied to me really quickly and told me to stay strong. They gave me a lot of numbers to ring, however I'd already called them. I felt that I was beginning to run out of ideas.

Michael had one final psychiatrist's appointment before the court. One step forward, two steps back, came to mind.

Michael's mental health deteriorated. He locked himself away. Here we were again, back in hell. I spoke to Michael on the phone and I could tell he'd been crying and he didn't want me to go round to see him.

I took Kian the autistic boy who I look after out for the day, as I knew I couldn't cancel that as he loved me to take him out. So I put on a brave face and with a broken heart we went to 'Play Zone' for the afternoon.

The three foster children also had a lovely day with

their mum. When the foster children came home it was shower time and time for bed. My husband stayed in whilst I took the little autistic boy home. When I'd dropped him off, I sat in my car and thought I'd give Michael a call but he didn't answer!

I rang again… and again.

My God, why wasn't he answering me?

My heart started racing and tears filled my eyes.

Why do we always have to have assessments? Even his doctor had changed his medication, as it wasn't working as well as he'd hoped. We were back in crisis!

I had to ring the out of hours mental team and told them that the doctor had changed his medication and he had crashed and wouldn't answer his phone. I was sweating and had a tight chest. I thought I was going to have a heart attack there and then. The lovely lady told me she was going to ring the police for assistance and advised me not to go into his flat but to wait outside.

Oh my God! They were thinking the worst.

How could I live without him?

Please be okay, I repeated over and over in my head as I drove as fast as I could to his flat!

I couldn't wait for the police. As soon as I got there I started banging on the door. But I couldn't get in as the key was in the lock on the inside. A few minutes later Michael came to the door. Once he opened it, I could see he was a wreck. He was crying and saying he couldn't cope anymore. He told me his phone had died. A few seconds later, the Police rang me and told me they were on their way.

I told them that Michael was okay and I was going to stay with him. I thanked them and advised them not to come. With that the mental health nurse called and spoke to Michael on the phone. My heart was breaking as I listened to Michael sobbing. The nurse then spoke to me and I promised I would arrange an emergency appointment with the doctor for the next morning.

Michael told me he would go with his dad as it distressed him even more to see me upset. So his dad took him and the doctor advised it was the change in the medication and also the assessment what has caused this, however he should stick with it as it would eventually make him feel better, and put him back on sick.

I will fight anyone who wants to assess him. Enough is enough. People often do not claim what they are entitled to because of the stress and anxiety - it just isn't worth it.

Why does everyone want to assess him? There should be a new law, that one assessment does all. Doesn't the government realise talking about it again and again is enough to send anyone crazy. PTSD had decided to take Michael's brain, to me it belonged in hell.

In November 2016, two and a half years after the accident, I read in our local paper that Owen's dad had been killed on his pushbike by a speeding lorry, in the same area where Owen had died.

It brought Owen's story flooding back again. One step forward, two steps back!

Michael went downhill as the guilt overflowed in him.

"Now his mum has no one," he'd say.

Sue Jorgensen

But I didn't feel sorry for them. The hate and the anger was still eating at me like a cancer and I knew I needed to see somebody before I went mad. I started attending counselling because I needed to find forgiveness for Owen and his family…

CHAPTER 5
MICHAEL AND LARISSA

In the spring of 2017, three years after the accident, whilst Michael was working on the tills at Asda, he met a lovely girl called Larissa with two lovely daughters. She was ex-army and she knew about PTSD but it didn't put her off. They've been together ever since although he still has his own flat while she owns her own house.

We learnt that when Michael was in a bad place we had to leave him and when he was feeling better we could return. She was okay with that as he didn't want anyone to see him in his dark and sad times.

I often found myself saying to Michael, 'See you're not worthless, horrible or scum because we love you, she loves you and those two little girls, absolutely adore you. You need to know that you are beautiful, inside and out, and we just lost you to PTSD.'

He gave me a little cheeky smile, and I said, 'Kids are good judges of character and they love you, so you are worth being loved.'

The doctor changed his medication and I have seen an improvement, he will never be who he was but I have to accept and love what he is now.

In the autumn of 2017 Larissa learned that she was

pregnant with Michael's baby. He had always wanted to be a dad and he was very excited. It was my first grandchild.

It wasn't easy for him in the beginning. At first he kept saying, "What if there's something wrong with it? Nothing good ever happens to me so this might not go right."

After all the scans however, he felt a bit more assured that things would be all right.

It was going to be a long journey to recovery but I had hope and faith.

I was still distant with my siblings and still trying to forgive Owen and his friend but the anger was getting less, which I was pleased about. I thought that when I read Owen's mum's book 'Smile', maybe the forgiveness might follow.

Reading back my story I realised that I'd changed and sometimes I may be a little mad and not very Christian. I know forgiveness is the only way but after seeing the lovely lady at Citizen's Advice and hearing her story I know God was listening to my prayers and helping me to look at both sides of things.

I'd written this book to help people understand more about PTSD and how it could produce a ripple effect and have an impact on whole families, not just the person who suffered the trauma.

When I was with my counsellor, Keith, after my usual ranting and raving, I told him I'd bought the book 'Smile' so that I could make peace with Owen. Then whilst I was chuntering he suggested that I write my own story, which helped me loads. I'm dyslectic and it was very hard for me to write it - and only I could read it with stuff back to front and a bit all over the shop. So I asked somebody at the church if they would type the first part up for me. I didn't want my husband to do it as I didn't want him to read it until it was finished and legible and then I would let him in to my and Michael's dark world.

When I was writing my book and when I bought the book 'Smile' I thought maybe God had a plan for me. Maybe this was my fate - to share my story. I even thought about the lad who had killed Owen's dad and how his family were coping and I hoped his mum has someone to talk to because it is dark and lonely if not. The poor lad didn't go out thinking I'll kill someone today, the same as Owen didn't set out thinking I'll destroy someone's life today.

What was again strange, was that I still didn't feel anything for Owen or his mum. Should I have been forgiving myself for being so wicked? All I wanted was my old son back. The happy, smiling and joking one, who had a good job, his own flat and paid all his own bills, and didn't have a worry in the world.

I had my faith, but that was now being tested, and I had my new son, the one with the parasite PTSD, torturing his brain. I grieved for my 'old' son and I had now accepted the changed one, the one that cried, sobbed, self harmed, took cannabis and drank. The one who didn't sleep and eat properly or keep himself clean. The one who hated himself and perceived himself as worthless and guilty scum. But he was none of these, not to me. He was my son and now he was a broken man...

Sue Jorgensen

For the three years since the accident I'd cooked and cleaned for Michael. The neighbours saw me all the time and they laughed and joked as they watched me clearing out his flat. But they never knew anything. In the beginning it was constant but as time went on things got better and now it was not every day like it used to be.

We had all learnt that we had to leave him be until the dark times passed, as the last thing he wanted to see was me or his girlfriend and children crying.

Larissa wanted him to move in with her full time but he was scared to, as he needed his sanctuary and he didn't want his new family to see him when he was in a bad place.

He even said to me one day, "What if my baby doesn't like me?"

I laughed and said, "The baby will adore you like nothing you've ever felt before as it's your baby and you will never feel love like it. When you first see him the bond will just hit you and it will be so unreal."

With me being a foster parent we had always had children with us so my birth children were used to having children around and sharing the love. But when Michael used to turn up he'd chase them around the house with spiders and they'd run around screaming. I'd tell him off and he'd then chase me with them. Then his sister would tell him off and it would be her turn. He chased us all apart from his dad, as he wasn't frightened of spiders.

So he would be an amazing and fantastic dad to his son as he was already an amazing step-dad to the two little girls. He still had very low self-esteem, though. If only he could see what we saw. And that was our job - to help make that happen...

At the beginning of 2018 – nearly a year since meeting Larissa and also having his medication changed - I noticed that Michael had a sparkle of hope in his eyes.

Was this it? Were we turning a corner? Was he slowly recovering? It was almost four years since the accident and it was the first time I was getting hopeful.

His girlfriend and her two little girls adored him so he was worth something. The kids sensed he was a good person and their love for him was unconditional.

"See, you are beautiful," I told him, "And you have a beautiful soul and people should think themselves very lucky to have you in their lives."

I'd spoken to his psychiatrist about him smoking cannabis and he didn't seem worried about it and said lots of people in Michael's situation smoke it to help them sleep. But although the psychiatrist wasn't concerned, I was worried about it...

CHAPTER 6
I FELT SO HELPLESS

When Michael was having a bad week he didn't go to work and so he didn't get paid but I was told that he should be able to get a top up due to his mental illness. I decided to find out and went to Citizens' Advice but there was a four-hour waiting time and I only wanted to ask a question and I had to get to work. I decided to go to a different one and went there the week after. There was only one member of staff and I was number '20' in the queue and it closed at 12 o'clock, so I went really early the next week.

I got there at 8.45am. There was a lady just in front of me. It had been throwing it down outside, I got the first ticket but I decided to give number one to the lady who was slightly in front of me.

I suggested getting a drink, but she replied, "I can't, I haven't any money."

I said that the drink was on me. What's 60p?

She was really grateful and started to tell me her story. She asked if I'd seen the story in the news about a boy on a motorbike that went missing? They'd found his body two days later in a ditch.

I said that I had and she explained that the boy was her son and the police said he wasn't speeding or he would have ended up in the field. It looked like he'd skidded, and that was why they think he'd been killed.

We started sharing each other's stories. I told her how I resented Owen and his family and how I was trying to forgive them but couldn't until Michael was better. We hugged each other and she told be that everyone was on her back for money. She owed money for the funeral and told me how she was suffering night terrors and how she wanted to break through the glass to hold her son at the mortuary. For that split second I felt a little bit sad for Owen's mum, as I knew she hadn't been allowed to see him as he was in a closed casket. That was the first time I'd ever felt anything for Owen's family.

We hugged again and said our goodbyes and I couldn't help thinking, did God bring us together to share our stories?

Later, I couldn't help thinking about her. Not only had she lost her son, but she also had debt collectors knocking at her door, as the bloody government hadn't given her enough to bury him.

I decided to look her up in the local paper and on the Internet to find out her address and decided to trace her the next day. I found the street where she lived and parked up and thought I'd ask someone. Somebody was bound to know who she was.

A couple walked past my car and I asked if they knew the lady and they replied, "Yes."

I couldn't believe it. I had parked right outside her house. Was that also fate? I knocked on the door and she answered. She looked a little surprised to see me but invited me in and I told her that I thought we were meant to have met and to share our stories. I also told her that I couldn't believe that despite her situation, debt collectors were on her back. I gave her £100. I know it wasn't much but I told her to do what she wanted with it. To either fill her cupboards or put it towards the debt.

"I wish I could give you more," I said.

She didn't want to take it but I persuaded her to, as she had given me hope that one day I might forgive Owen.

It was also early in 2018, nearly four years after the accident, that I found out that Michael might be entitled to PIP - Personal Independents Payment - as his wages fluctuated depending on his state of mind?

Why hadn't anyone told us this?

He had been getting help towards his council tax and rent and his dad and me often put money in his bank to cover car insurance and MOT. I was sure he would pay us it back when his compensation came through. But there was a chance that this would be going to court - and what price would you put on someone's head 'being fucked' – whatever happened, we just had to learn to live with it.

God knows all the treatment he'd had but the parasite was still there, refusing to leave. It had already been nearly four years and it would take 'as long as it takes'.

I just hoped he would get enough to make sure he was never homeless. I didn't think Social Services would let him move back home with me as I had three foster children. And I didn't want them to see him at his worst, they only saw him at his best. I had to protect the children. That's why I knew he would never move back home anyway, as he always tried to protect people from his black moods and I think that was also why he wouldn't move in with Larissa. However, one day when things get easier and his PTSD is less severe, and he is busy with the baby, then things may be more normal and he won't need his sanctuary.

I told Larissa that she'd saved him. She's a lovely strong person, just what he needed, and a fantastic mum to the girls.

I'd planned to go to Tenerife with my friend Jackie a few weeks later, to heal my mind and read the book 'Smile' and find out all about Owen.

I hoped that forgiveness would follow. I thought that I might even send Owen's mum a copy of my book, so that she could read what we had been through. Then I thought that perhaps that wouldn't be the right thing to do but I would decide when it was printed.

I asked at the church that I attend and a lovely lady offered to type it up for me. I told her that I didn't want anyone to read it until it was finished and ready to be published.

I was also worried that if it did go to court what effect it would have on Michael and would we have to relive it again and would it take us back to square one?

As far as I was aware he had stopped self harming and putting pins down his nails. And if he was burning or cutting himself I was sure that Larissa would notice and she'd tell me.

One of the big changes in Michael was that he couldn't cope with any sort of stress no matter how small. He couldn't even answer the phone if he didn't recognise the number.

He had never even spoken to the solicitor or seen her,

as it would have caused a panic attack.

He couldn't deal with anything.

He became stressed about bills, the rent, doctors, the bank and the assessments for his mental health; it all just stressed him out.

His dad kept telling me I needed to give him some responsibilities back, as it would aid his recovery. I tried, but things didn't get paid on time, then his stress levels would rise.

He then said that he didn't care and he would rather be homeless, as he couldn't cope with the stress. I could understand that, especially if he hadn't had any sleep for a week.

I know people who told me that they knew about PTSD but unless you've lived with it or know someone with the condition you will never know what it is like.

I felt hopeless, useless, and didn't know what I was supposed to do to help him to try and pull him out of it.

I tried the soft approach, the hard approach, the listening to his anger.

I didn't get a manual on how to deal with it. I wish there'd been a manual on how to save your son or daughter with PTSD as I needed it.

At times his mental state was so bad I would try to drag him to the doctors but he would refuse as he thought he deserved all the pain and suffering. He would shout and swear in my face and beg me to punch him and kick him. Then I'd start crying and say 'I can't hurt you, you're my son.'

He would throw me out and again I would ring the mental health. But unless he rang them, they couldn't help.

THE RIPPLE EFFECT

For him, he thought he deserved the mental torture as he had killed someone and left that person's parents childless. The guilt he felt for that was unbearable and for a mother to watch her son who she loved dearly, crumble in front of her eyes was horrendous.

I felt helpless, watching him suffer.

A doctor hadn't diagnosed me but my counsellor thought I was suffering from secondary trauma syndrome. I read up on this and I agreed with him. I could close my eyes and I was there at the accident. I knew all the graphic details. I could see all his nightmares and I wasn't even there in body. I just wished that Michael could have turned it around, and thought; they were in the wrong, he killed himself and he could have killed me.

That's what I think I would have done. I would have turned my thoughts around and tried not to let it eat me up like a cancer. That's what I'd like to think I'd have been like. But the police told me that Michael had witnessed one of the worst accidents they had ever been to.

Michael used to have a reaction to a certain smell that used to make him want to vomit. We went through a list including oil, burning rubber and petrol, but we couldn't put our finger on the smell until a bag of meat split on his till and the blood seeped out and he had a panic attack. It was the iron in the blood that was a trigger…

CHAPTER 7
IF YOU'RE LISTENING GOD

I don't think I will ever be the same with my siblings as not one of my brothers was there for Michael or me and even though they didn't know the full impact of what was happening, not one of them looked out for him. Someone could have put out an olive branch out to him to get him to go to the house parties but nobody did. They just partied on and left us out of it.

I'd no ill feelings towards my eldest sister as she had her reasons and own problems. She was left with a broken heart when her husband Owen passed away suddenly with only four days' notice. He was an amazing man, bless his soul. I talked to her now and again afterwards, and I shed tears for Michael and she shed tears for her husband.

The people I spoke to were my niece Amie and my friends, Jackie and Marion, but they never knew the full impact it had on me.

I felt as if I was getting tortured myself as I couldn't get the help for Michael and I always hit a brick wall.

I don't think the government and mental health understand that most mental health patients do not want to ring as they think they deserve their punishment. It's the same with the doctors. He wasn't going to go to see the doctor when he was in a bad way as it was never the same doctor and he had to start to explain everything again from the beginning.

You would ring at 8am in the morning and it was engaged. Then once you got through you had to wait two weeks. You also had the walk in clinics where the staff didn't know your background and you ended up going round in circles. The NHS is overworked and bursting at the seams.

I had never prayed for money and wealth, I think we should live and be happy with what we have. That was until the accident happened. Then I prayed time and time again to win the lottery so I could send Michael away to a private clinic, either here or abroad, to deal with his PTSD.

So yes, I did wish to win the lottery, so that I could pay for that woman's funeral, make sure Michael was safe and secure and start a group for PTSD that anyone could attend, not just soldiers. My children are my world and one of them was suffering and broken.

I had my three beautiful foster children who I cared for and I also had my part-time jobs looking after people. I gave as much as I could, in fact at times I didn't know how I did it. I think I had been in robot mode. I also had my beautiful daughter who I felt was neglected as she lives in Scotland and it had always been about Michael.

It was like being on a rota. Michael got me from 9 till 3.30, then my children came home from school and got my attention. Then my husband got home from work and once my children were in bed, Michael had me for the rest of the time if he needed me, sending me a message back to let me know he was okay. He never left me suffering and worrying again now that he knew he just had to send me a kiss.

I also have an anxiety trigger, if Michael rings me and I can't answer when I'm driving and he then rings again straight after that, I start to panic and feel sick and I'm frightened to ring him back. So we now have an arrangement that if I don't answer he will text me instead and we can talk as soon as I am able to do so.

I really hope Owen's mum reads this if I get it sorted so she realises what we've gone through. I know she lost her son and husband and I can't imagine what she has been going through, but I have had to watch mine being tortured every day of his life.

The only way I can explain it is if you had two children and one could be taken quickly and the other one stayed alive but was then continuously cut with a knife. Which end would you choose for your child?

People might think that we had just carried on but we had been living through hell. I hoped that one day Owen's mum would meet up with me but she might hate me for the things I had said but this is how it had been and how I felt.

As for the government, they don't understand about any of this. They don't understand mental health. Unless you've been part of it and lived through it, you don't understand it. Lots of times I had felt like ringing the mental health team and screaming at them, "Well, he's not going to ring and talk to you as he's done all that in counselling."

I just wanted someone to turn up and section him.

Then it entered my head again to contact Russell Brand and ask for his help. I didn't hold out much hope for the PIP as I'd been told that 'if you couldn't see it, you're fucked' - and you couldn't see into someone's brain.

I'd never been bothered about money but if I'd been rich he would be being looked after now. His bags would be packed and he would have been sent to a private clinic, preferably in America. I would buy him a house and he would never be homeless and all his bills would be paid and he wouldn't have to worry about anything. So if you are listening God I would like to win the lottery but not for personal gain, so I can start this support group so those who suffer can help one another as this is what Michael has always wanted.

He told me that I was the worst counsellor as I always started crying, even though I tried to hold it back.

In early 2018 Sharma came home from Scotland on a surprise visit. I couldn't help feeling guilty as the last four years had been all about Michael. I wanted to make it up to her as I love her to bits and she never complained that she didn't have any of my time, bless her. She had worked so hard and would soon become a qualified disability nurse. I was so proud of her. She had caught me crying a couple of times even though I tried to hide my sadness as best I could. But she's not daft, although she doesn't say anything. She knows I love them both the same but at the moment one of them was broken and needed fixing and there only seemed to be me that could try and make him better.

PTSD has two sides to it, the one where it is leaving you alone - and then the side when thoughts jump in and you are screaming inside whilst it's torturing your brain. My son lives with this - it must be unbearable.

Four years have been clouded because of 'that day'. I've started to work out the signs on a bad day. If Michael was covering his face with his hood and being very quiet, then he had probably been awake most of the night with night terrors. If he was sitting talking normally but his hands and legs were tapping, his anxiety levels were through the roof.

The guilt brought self harm and it was always the same thing, pins down his nails or the pointed end of sharp knives or the last one was anger where he was crying, shouting, swearing and asking me to hit him or bash him with a pan or something.

When he got all five together, Oh my God!

We had weeks of dark times and it took a while to get him out of the dark place. But he knew he has to send me a text, even if it was just a kiss to let me know he was alive.

It was unbelievable!

In February 2018, just a day before my week's holiday with Jackie, it was all over the local paper again. The person who'd had the accident with Owen's dad had been to court. The lad got six months in prison and a three-year ban but of course it brought up Owen's story and his face was in the paper again.

I really hoped Michael didn't see it and realised that Owen's mum wouldn't have had any say in it going in the newspaper, as it was news.

People were complaining about the short sentence that the lad received. But all I could think of was that I knew someone whose dangerous driving had caused the death of one person and another to suffer with PTSD, and nothing at all had happened to them.

I hoped to God that Michael didn't see it in the paper, as the last thing he needed was to see Owen's face.

I made his dad aware of it and kept an eye out. I was actually thinking about going to see the lad in prison just to tell him not to be so hard on himself as it was an accident. If his mum was anything like me she would need to talk to someone instead of going insane as no one wanted to see their son suffer and I was sure that he would be fighting his demons like my son.

It had been almost four years since the accident and the story was still going in the paper every year. I wouldn't have minded if it was just about the dad, but why did they always have to put Owen in too? Michael was not at work that day so hopefully he wouldn't see it unless someone told him about it.

I also found out in 2018 that Michael could be entitled to IIDB -Industrial Industries Disablement Benefit - I'd never heard of it. And no surprise here, they advised me that they needed to do an assessment!

I'm going to send a copy of my story to the Prime Minister to show how ridiculous the government is. I know I'm repeating myself but this is how my brain repeats, trying to make sense of it all. I do really believe the wealthy with mental health get all the help they need because money talks. But we minions have to fight for everything. God knows how I fought, so that the ripple effect stopped at me.

It was nearly four years and my boy was still broken. I could only hope and pray that it got easier for us both…

CHAPTER 8
TENERIFE

In February 2018 I went on holiday to Tenerife as planned with my best friend Jackie. Whilst I was there I started to read Tracey Milner's book 'Smile' and it really cheesed me off.

All the support and help she received from the police and the army, and we got nothing. The police only came twice to Michael's flat, once was to take his statement and the second to tell him that someone had been arrested and to give him his mobile phone back.

They also took me aside and said that Michael would need therapy and told me that they had quite a few witnesses to say the car and the motorbike had been racing but they were not going to press charges as the car driver had to live with the loss of his best friend. I think it also helped that he was in the army and on army leave.

I was so angry, it had to be true, all the witnesses were not going to lie. The only time they didn't race was when they were going through the town. I'm going with the witnesses statements, that's what set me up for years, my son had been tortured for years and the car driver got nothing. How was that fair? Owen lost his life, but my son who saw everything was left with PTSD. It was only six months before that I'd asked

Michael if he wanted me to find out how he had got away with it.

Michael hugged me and replied, "No, how do you know he's not like me?"

I told Michael I couldn't forgive Owen for making him ill and making him so sad and he kissed me on the head and said, "I forgive him mum, he has lost his life and I hope someday I will get better. I will never forget it. I will just live with it."

That was when I started to think I needed to change my mindset and find forgiveness. I prayed again to God and asked for guidance.

I bumped into the lady at Citizen's Advice, I've read the book 'Smile'. I cannot believe how Owen and Michael are so much alike, reading that book was like reading about Michael before the accident and the difference between our two families, we just got left to rot with no support.

In the book it said that Michael received a letter from Owen's mum and dad, although I'm almost certain we didn't receive it. But there is a copy of it in the book and one day maybe I will let Michael read it.

Why didn't Owen's family ask us if there was anything they could do to help Michael? I wanted to find and help the mother and the lad who killed Owen's father as I didn't want her to be like me with no support.

I know Owen's mum had been grieving for her son; but I'd been fighting for mine to help him stay alive and to fight his PTSD. Will he have this torture forever?

Owen's mum actually talked about 'the ripple effect' in her book. I thought that was really strange, as that was what I was going to call my book. She also talked about us bumping into one another in the court, but we had actually bumped into one another in the toilet and she told me how worried she was about Owen's friend.

I wanted to scream at her, "What about my son? What about the mess this had left my son in?"

I wanted to punch her in the face and shout at her, "Are you crazy woman? Have you seen what they've done to my son? They've left him broken. He is a shell of himself. He doesn't sleep for days. And you weren't told the full details of the accident like we were. Are you stupid?"

It was there in black and white, the facts were there! They were racing! But in the book it was sugar-coated, as not once did it say that they were racing. But I didn't say anything about that. I just said he would be okay.

Michael looked into Owen's eyes and that is what haunted him and the horrors of what he saw when he went to help him. No one else knew, just Michael and me.

After nearly four years, we were gradually seeing a slight change in Michael. We even saw a smile sometimes and now that he was going to be a dad he was very excited, even though because of his low self-esteem, he thought the baby wouldn't like him. I asked him why he thought that he wouldn't like him, you are a beautiful person, everyone loves you, Larissa's girls adore you so why wouldn't your son?

My first grandchild was due on May 3rd 2018, so there were changes on the way for the better. I planned to find Owen's grave and lay the flowers and tell him I forgave him and I hoped he could forgive me for hating him.

THE RIPPLE EFFECT

I do believe in the afterlife and that your body is just a shell carrying the soul and they will be up there doing whatever they do. I was finally letting go of my anger, loathing and hate. I was thinking that all my emotions were keeping him in limbo and not letting him move on, which made me feel I had the power and control. How wicked was that, me holding on to his soul?

Once I laid the flowers I let go and made my peace.

I love my son as much as Owen's mum loved her son. But he was at rest and mine was still in pain. If he had received the letter she talked about in the book, maybe it would have helped. But I don't think it was forwarded on, which was a real shame.

Don't ever think that it was just Owen who died that day because my son did too.

Counselling had helped my grief and helped me to cope with Michael, so both Owen's mum and I have grieved in different ways. Her son was dead and gone but my son was still here. And I hoped that a new baby and me being able to forgive Owen might help us to heal as a family.

My husband is different to us, he is so laid back, he never shows anger or hatred, he is placid and peaceful and always says life has a plan for us all and there are things we need to learn. I keep a lot to myself, as no one else needs to suffer like us.

Michael had Larissa and a baby on the way, and life seemed to be getting better for him. He couldn't give up his flat as he still needed a safe haven but hopefully he will move on in time and finally live the life he had always wanted.

It was a strange day but my mind was now clearer. I

wish I'd received the letter, she did care about my son. I only wish I'd asked her to help bring my son back as I know it had been eating away at me.

The last four years had been the longest four years of my life. I accepted that my son would never be the same again, but I love and cherish him for who he is now, my beautiful son who deserved to be happy - and I didn't want to hold him back. I needed to let go and if I can help anyone whose child suffers with PTSD with this story then it was a good thing. PTSD doesn't usually end in death, it ripples and tries to destroy everyone involved.

Sitting there in Tenerife, I realised I'd also been angry with God. How could he do this to us? We were good people who tried to help others, yet He'd put my son through mental torture. But slowly my faith was returning and I was starting to see some rays of light through the dark.

I also realised that I'd never told my counsellor that I was a foster carer. Maybe because I wanted to keep my 'two lives separate. The children didn't know anything, they didn't even know there was an accident, as they deserved the best from me.

Social Services knew I was having counselling and they were happy I was getting support dealing with a son with PTSD. I felt I was making peace with everything, even my siblings. Maybe I'd kept too much to myself. I didn't realise the hell that Michael and I were in.

My best friend Jackie was surprised how much I

slept on holiday. Every time I closed my eyes I fell asleep. It was the first time my brain was not working overtime and trying to make sense of what happened to my son. I'd never felt so relaxed at any time in the last four years.

I rang Michael and he sounded okay. I don't think he'd seen the paper so maybe time was the great healer.

One night whilst we were in Tenerife, we went to see a show. They sang an Abba song and just at that moment I realised that I was no longer angry with God. I still had my faith and what a fantastic feeling that was. Yes, I'd had a few glasses of wine, but the words "I believe in Angels" had hit me like lightning. Had he heard my prayers all the time and was this just my path?

I realised how much I loved life and that Michael would learn to love life again too. We all have beginnings and endings to our journeys and the start of his journey to recovery had just begun.

It felt good to feel positive and I hoped I'd be able to pass on my strength to Michael.

It was one of the best things I'd done, to get away with my friend and find myself and clear my mind. My shoulders were light and I was ready to face the future. We'd beat this PTSD together. God, I was feeling strong. I just wished I'd got that bloody letter. That would have made life easier. I still wasn't going to mention it to Michael though in case guilt kicked in. I still actually felt a bit mean, feeling nothing for that family but anger and hate.

Jackie kept telling me, 'She's lost her son, you need to forgive.' But I just couldn't do it.

I know that Michael received one letter from the

couple who looked after him at the scene. But I just couldn't stop racking my brain and trying to remember if we received the other one.

I slept so much on the holiday. I think my brain was worn out and it needed to recharge. But I felt great and maybe it was because it was the longest time – two weeks - that Michael had been without a bad day that helped. Was this a turning point? I really hoped so.

He was really excited about the baby being born. Maybe he was realising that he could be happy and he deserved to be happy. And the biggest thing – had he realised the accident wasn't his fault, there was nothing he could have done about it and what a tragedy it was for everyone involved?

I know that a fortnight of being normal might not seem much to some people but it was a miracle for us. Two whole weeks without any mental torture - it must have been bliss for him…

CHAPTER 9
A MOTHER'S DAY TRIP

Monday March 5th was a very strange day.

Michael and Larissa and the girls came round for tea. I was cutting Michael's hair and I asked him if he'd ever received a letter from Owen's mum? He said, "Yes," but it had taken him a while to read it. He asked me why? And I told him I couldn't remember him getting the letter. The only one I could remember was from the people who had looked after him at the accident. I said that I hadn't seen Owen's mum's letter, and asked him if he was getting confused? He replied that he didn't know. I also told him I was going to find Owen's grave and lay some flowers, as it was a way to find closure and forgiveness.

Michael hugged me and said, "Good, so you should."

I asked if he wanted to come with me? He looked at me and his heartbeat changed. He started to well up and said that he would like to but it might be too soon. I could see an attack coming on so I stopped talking about it.

Before he left, I said, 'If you want to, I'll take you on Monday and maybe it will be closure for you before your son arrives. I will let you decide, it has to be when you're feeling strong enough.'

His dad thought that Michael and Larissa should go on their own because we were not good for each other, as we would be too emotional, but he definitely needed closure. And I could now see the light at the end of the very dark tunnel.

I was at my therapist today for a very long talk, even though I do most of it, even Keith can see the change in me. I told him in the beginning I wanted him to tell me answers and tell me what to do. He didn't give me any of that, he just listened to me ranting and raving. I told him I would have done anything he told me to help Michael.

He smiled at me and said I was getting there on my own and making sense of it, which was great to see. He said he was here to help me to work things out.

I was going to miss him. It had gone from once every two weeks to once a month, this was how far I'd come.

Although the accident and the PTSD was going to be with us forever, hopefully one day it would turn out to be just a distant memory.

I'd written a letter to Owen's mum, telling her how it had been for us. The beginning seemed quite harsh but I planned to hand it to the vicar with my phone number, so if she wanted to get in touch, she could. I'd see what happened on the Sunday when I took the flowers but I didn't even know if the vicar would be there.

On March 11th 2018, Mother's Day, I went to the cemetery in Driffield to make peace with Owen and try to find forgiveness. My anger had actually gone and it was time to move on. I really believed that meeting the lady at Citizens Advice was my turning point. She would never know how much she had helped me and I just hoped I could win the lottery so I could help her to find peace.

The information I had was what I'd found out myself. There were three churches in Driffield, one Catholic, one Methodist and one Church of England. By reading the book I thought she was a Christian, so I started off at All Saints. It was a really beautiful day, the sun was shining and I already felt at peace.

My husband and I walked around but there was no sign of a cemetery. A lady walked past and I asked her where the cemetery was? She explained it was about a five-minute walk away. I also asked where the vicarage was and she pointed to a hall and said we could get a cup of tea or coffee there. She told us to go with her and she'd introduce me to the vicar, which I did whilst my husband stayed by the car. I asked the vicar if I could have a quiet word and he took me to a side room. I told him I wanted to pass on my letter and make peace. I needed to tell Owen's mum that I had read the book and I was giving her some information, as she wanted to know how Michael was doing.

He told me he hadn't taken that funeral but looked in a book and said the vicar who had conducted it had since retired but they still talked on the phone and he would pass it on so Owen's mum would receive it. I told him it was very private and asked him to let me know when he had handed it over. I thanked him very much and left.

Back in the car I wasn't sure I'd done the right thing as the beginning of the letter was quite harsh but it got better. I hoped she understood that I had to do it for closure. I looked out of the window of the car as we made our way to the cemetery. We parked at the side of the road and Gerald squeezed my leg and asked if I was okay. He said we needed to look at the newer part of the cemetery, which was right at the very back. He started at one side and I started at the other, walking up and down, looking at the names on the gravestones. After about ten minutes I found his name and I shouted my husband across, all the hairs on my arms were standing up, I wanted to cry but I held it back as I didn't want my husband to see, I sorted out the flowers but asked my husband to leave me to talk and I needed time on my own to talk to Owen. As the guilt of being so unforgiving hit me, my husband asked if I was okay?

I replied, "Yes," and he slowly walked away.

I stood there for a few minutes. It was like traffic on a motorway speeding through my mind with all the horrible things I'd said and there I was standing at the grave.

Tears filled my eyes and I stared apologising and asking Owen to forgive me for having control of his soul.

I thought that now he was free as I had forgiven him.

How could I have been so mean and hateful after he had lost his life? That was not who I am and you can never move on without forgiveness, so I said I was sorry and that to me his soul was now free as I forgived him. It may sound stupid but that was how I felt.

I held the tears back and walked away from the grave, which was totally different to how I expected it to be. It was right at the very back of the graveyard with a very small headstone. My husband Gerald explained that it was an army grave. We talked a little and then he took me for dinner.

It was a strange day, how things fell into place. I knew I wouldn't see Michael as he was working that day. We'd always encouraged him to go to work even on a bad day. I arrived home at 3.30 and waited for my foster children to come home. They had spent the day with their mum, and as soon as they arrived home they excitedly told me what they'd done.

I cooked our tea then sent them for a shower as it was school the next day. My husband stayed in with the kids after tea and I popped to my mum's to take her Mother's day gift. Before I left, Gerald again asked me if I was feeling okay and I again said, 'Yes.'

Whilst I was out, Michael had turned up and brought me a card and a bottle of 'Baileys' and my daughter had sent me a card and some flowers from Scotland.

I rang Michael when I got back to thank him. I could tell by his voice that there was something wrong and I asked him if he was okay. He said he was having a few bad days and I could tell that he was trying not to cry on the phone.

Of course, it was Mother's Day. That was when his guilt kicked in. I didn't think. I talked normally to him but he said he needed to go. I said I would text him later and see him the next day. I had been that involved in myself and I forgot it was a bad time for Michael. It was the time when he overloaded with guilt for Owen's mum. I spoke to Larissa and she said he hadn't been round and she knew he was in a bad place. The thing was that he didn't like his family to see him sad.

What surprised me though, was how his sadness

didn't affect me as much as it used to, so maybe that was me getting used to the idea. I knew he hated it when I got upset.

How stupid was I, forgetting that it was such a difficult time for him? I just didn't think. I was so wrapped up in myself. But that must have meant I was recovering. So, if I was recovering, there was hope for Michael.

I told his dad that Michael was upset, and that I could tell it in his voice. His dad looked up at me and said he didn't want to tell me but Michael had turned up in a right state and my husband had comforted him and they'd had a long talk.

Michael pulled himself together but Gerald hadn't wanted to tell me about it, as it had been the day I'd finally made my peace with Owen...

The last four years had been unbelievably hard, especially keeping everything between just Michael and me. I was so sad that I'd started to lose my faith. I still prayed for guidance and I believed that I was being heard now.

Hopefully my son's illness would mellow. It would never leave him but maybe he could make peace with himself, as he now had a little family like he'd always wanted...

CHAPTER 10
I JUST HAD TO KEEP FIGHTING

What a strange day today, the solicitors have rung me and they have had a meeting about Michael and they are worried about the stress it will cause him if it has to go to court. I agreed with them. They are going to sort out an assessment with a physiatrist and psychologist together and they will pass the report onto the solicitor and then the other solicitor and maybe they will sort this out of court. I told the solicitor that I wasn't going to tell Michael the court date until the day before as I didn't want him spiralling downwards but hopefully it wouldn't come to that.

The solicitor asked me why Michael wasn't available in May in case they sent us an assessment date for then and I explained his sister was coming home again for a few days and that the baby was due in May. She sounded surprised but I thought she already knew that Michael was going to be a dad. Maybe I didn't tell her. Maybe I wanted to keep the happy news to ourselves.

I didn't tell Michael any of the conversations we had, as he would have just worried. Also today, what pissed me off was PIP. They said they wanted to see him next week. I wasn't happy about that, they'd already got psychiatrists' reports and all that was needed. Why did they need to see him?

I'd already told him that he was getting another appointment to see another physiatrist and that I would pass on that report, so I didn't understand why they needed to see him. How many more times did he need to go through it?

I rang and told them I didn't think it was appropriate to visit when they were getting the next report. Were people trying to push him over the edge? They put me through to another department and I was on hold for thirty minutes. It closed at six and it was already ten past, so I put the phone down as no one was going to answer.

I thought I'd tell Michael on the Wednesday as they were coming on the Thursday, so I rang them the next day and I told the lady on the phone my concerns. That he didn't like to talk to anyone or see anyone and I was thinking of cancelling the whole thing but she was quite good and said that he didn't have to talk to anyone as long as he was there, not even in the same room.

I actually said I felt like telling them to stick it where the sun didn't shine and we wouldn't bother but she reassured me that as long as he was there it didn't matter.

I hated having to tell Michael there were more meetings to attend.

God, I hate this government. It sucks when it comes to mental health. There is just too much pressure. No wonder so many people take their own lives. One thing I'd learnt living with a son with PTSD was you couldn't just let it go, as everyone wants to assess him and write reports and make you go over and over it. My God, I'd be glad when everyone just left him alone.

THE RIPPLE EFFECT

I knew PIP had to do their reports but my God they had all his information about his treatment and psychiatrists' reports - what more did they want, his blood?

Should I have just told them to shove it? Did I want this stress?

They couldn't look into his mind. Yes he could move his arms, yes he could move his legs and he could stand on his tiptoes. But no, sorry, he couldn't get out of bed, get washed, get dressed, clean, feed himself when he was having a bad week. So write that in your report!

In fact, he didn't go to work and didn't get paid; write that in your report!

God it really made me angry because the next lot of assessments were all done by top professionals. Had I to ring them the next day and tell them to stick it?

I was going to worry about it now until the next week. I didn't sleep properly with thinking about cancelling the appointment for the PIP assessments. What was the nurse going to do? I wasn't sure how Michael was going to feel. I'd be glad when it was all over. How could anybody move on with the constant reminders?

The following morning I went to see Helen who was typing the text of my book for me. Helen's a really lovely lady. She got a bit teary as I had to read out what I'd written. I got a bit choked up too. Time was passing and the tears kept flowing. I didn't realise how exhausting it would be and I'm sure she felt the same. But we got through a lot of it so decided to stop and continue the next day. I said my goodbyes and went to take my mum to a hospital appointment. See no one knows about my story apart from Gerald, Jackie and Helen.

My parents don't even know as they are in their seventies and this should be their happy times instead of having to worry about Michael. When they ask, I tell them very little and keep smiling. I've got really good at being okay as my foster kids are not aware of any of this either and are thriving, which brings me a lot of happiness. God bless them, they're amazing.

Michael said to me, "Anyone who has you in their life is really lucky because you're amazing, funny and full of love and me and Sharma are so blessed to have you as our mum. And dad is blessed to have met you." Sharma always says lovely things too and my foster children tell me they love me and give me cuddles all the time.

Even my husband tells me every day, 'God you're beautiful, I'm a lucky man, I love you.'

I am truly loved which is a blessing but you do love your children more than life itself and you take their pain if you can. One of mine was broken and when I begged for help nothing happened, so I just had to keep fighting.

I got a message saying that my letter had been posted through Owen's mum's door. I wasn't sure how I felt, the letter had sounded a bit harsh at the beginning but that was how it had been for us. But I did finish it on a positive note. Still, what is done is done - and it was a part of my closure.

On March 18th 2018 I emailed the solicitor to see if we could push for Michael's assessment with the PIP, either for the end of March or some time in April, as I didn't want anything upsetting him when the arrival of his son was due in early May. I just wanted Michael to focus on that and nothing else. I'd still not told him about the visit from PIP the following Thursday, as he would just worry and not sleep. I still didn't understand why they needed to see him. Still, the days were getting better, apart from Mother's Day.

I coped very well when Michael wasn't coping and I found out that because of his guilt, he was still self harming. But I was getting stronger to care for Michael. If I wasn't crying it was better for him.

I received another email from the solicitor on March 23rd 2018 saying we had a slot for court, a two-day trial, in 2019. That was a long way off bearing in mind it was to agree Michael's compensation settlement and to me nothing would be enough.

I just wished the accident hadn't happened and my son wasn't suffering with this mental illness but we can't change the past and because it is going to court I hope the judge is going to make the insurance company pay big time as my son is going to have to live through this again, shame on them.

If I get a chance to speak to the judge I will tell them that right after the accident we got a letter offering £1,000 off Owen's insurers saying they were sorry and asking him to sign some forms, the crafty bastards. If this had happened to someone else, with no family, not thinking, they would have signed their rights away, which makes them scum to me.

I said, "Bring it on, bring it on!"

So my story wasn't going to get an ending just yet as

it hadn't ended. But the reason for me writing it - that I wanted to share it with as many people as possible, and that PTSD isn't just for soldiers and anyone can suffer from it - made me more determined than ever to complete it.

I hadn't got a clue how I was going to get it published as a short story or if anyone would be interested in helping me to get it out there. If I did manage to get it published, any profit would go to make my son secure and pay the funeral costs for the lovely lady I'd met at CA. So my plan was to send it to people who I felt were genuine and who had the respect of the public as I felt that people would listen to them. Knowing my luck though, it would probably end up in the bin but maybe this time someone would listen and help me to get it out there.

I'd like to thank Helen as I know this wasn't easy for her, as I shed a few tears during this process and I saw her crying at times.

I'd like to end this chapter with something I read and it is so true…

The funny thing is nobody ever really knows how much someone is hurting.

We could be standing next to someone who is completely broken and we wouldn't even know it...

CHAPTER 11
MY FIRST GRANDCHILD

It hadn't been an easy nine-month ride as Michael's self-doubt and worrying about the baby made him quite anxious and worried. But on May 17th my first grandchild arrived, a whopping ten pound five. It was Michael's first child and we couldn't be happier. Elliot Michael, welcome to this crazy world. Elliot was here now and he loved his daddy very much and we loved him.

Michael's PTSD had been up and down for nearly four years. Would it ever leave us alone? The answer to that one was, No!

Then another surprise! He got a letter from PIP telling him that someone was coming to see him. He was really upset that someone was coming to the flat especially as I didn't tell him until the night before. He wouldn't come out of the room and he wouldn't even talk. The meeting turned out to be just to inform me that I would have control of the money if he was awarded it and Michael just had to sign some paperwork.

Another appointment had to be made for a home visit assessment. I didn't want this to happen but rules are rules and they needed to see him to do this. Even though all the psychiatrist and doctor's report statesd that this was not good for his mental condition. Again I didn't tell him until the night before as he would have been stressed and his anxiety would have hit the roof. I told Michael I would be at his flat the next morning as the appointment was for 9.30am.

When I arrived the next day I found that he'd been awake all night due to panic attacks. He told me he didn't want to speak to anybody as it would cause severe flashbacks, so I told him to go to his room and I'd speak on his behalf.

The 9.30 appointment came and went but when nobody had arrived by 12 o'clock, I rang the office. I was told they were not coming to do the assessment and that they wanted to re-arrange it. It was like a bomb exploding! I explained to them that Michael had been up all night self-harming and was a wreck.

I said, 'How could you do this to us? If I'd known this I wouldn't have told him and caused further emotional pain."

I'm sorry to say that I then swore!

'Are you fucking crazy?' I asked. 'Is there any wonder people commit suicide? I want to speak to a manager now!'

My poor Michael had been through all that stress again - and for nothing!

They apologised again and I told them to stick their apologies. That was not going to help his wounds to heal or his mental state. They said a manager would call, so I stayed with Michael for a while until he was calm.

When I arrived home the phone rang and it was the manager from PIP. She also apologised and said she had tried to call me, however I explained that I'd had no missed calls or answer messages, and that she should've kept trying, as this was someone's life at risk. I also explained that Michael wouldn't have had a meltdown if I hadn't told him about the meeting. So again the process started all over again from the beginning.

Why aren't a doctor's and psychiatrist's notes official? It was beyond me! I told the manager I wanted to make my complaint official. She typed this up and she apologised again. At this point I was furious. I told her to stick it and if that was how they treated people with mental health problems it was disgusting.

So an appointment was made for a week later. All I was thinking about was how was I going to tell Michael again. No wonder people didn't claim, as it was far too stressful. Tears filled my eyes and my brain was screaming. Where was the help? Did the government actually give a shit?

Two days before the next appointment I got a phone call from the assessment nurse, and she actually did the assessment with me over the phone. She did not want to see Michael!

Hallelujah! Someone was finally listening to me.

The next day I got a letter of apology, which I was not expecting. And eight weeks later he was awarded his PIP…

I remember being so angry one morning when I received a report from the defendants. Their doctor had read Michael's reports from his doctors and psychiatrist and this supposed doctor had then to write his own report about Michael.

All the parties involved had decided for Michael not

to have another assessment due to his mental health.

My God, I think this doctor needed to go back to medical school! He believed his PTSD was bad because his ex-girlfriend had cheated on him and that was why he kept relapsing!

What about the fact that it had been in the paper every single year? And why would his cheating ex-girlfriend cause panic attacks, anxiety attacks, triggers, noises and smells?

In fact this was my letter back to the solicitor:-

Dear Sally,

After reading the report I can honestly say Dr Smith needs to go back to medical school. I have never read so much rubbish, did he not read the reports?

Yes, Michael's ex-girlfriend cheated on him and his friend was ill. Yes, this is upsetting but this is life! And he won't be the first and he won't be the last to be cheated on.

Unfortunately, looking into someone's eyes so close that you can see the stubble on their face, then to go over and help out, only to find the flattened head still in the helmet with no body while his legs were still moving... that image would destroy anyone's life.

So as for Michael's relapse, maybe it didn't help that we couldn't get away from it as it has been in our local newspaper every year. I'm sending you copies look at the dates I have wrote on this only half of them. So Dr Smith's report was only good for the bin in my opinion.

I didn't show Michael the report as he was in a good place at that moment and I didn't want him stressed.

As for Michael's anxiety and panic attacks they come

and go on triggers, such as the smell of blood, the sound of loud motorbikes and certain songs that were playing in the cars that had stopped at the scene. That was only a few. So can Dr Smith explain to me why any of these triggers have anything to do with his ex-girlfriend? He wants to try and live in our shoes. It's been a living hell.

Sorry for my rant, but I was so angry. If Michael's doctor and Dr Jones are saying the same thing, what the hell is Dr Smith talking about? He had never met Michael and I think that you need proof he's a qualified doctor because I think he talks a load of tosh.

Thank you for your time.

Yours truly.

I rang the solicitor and even she was surprised at the report. I don't believe the doctor read the other reports. I even sent my solicitor all of the copies that had been in the paper. Even the charity events what Owen's mum had done. I really don't think she believes they were racing? Wasn't she listening to the witnesses? One witness said they were going that fast they went past like a blip. When the judge asked what a blip was, the witness replied that it passed that fast you could hardly see it.

Another witness said if he had pulled out in his car seconds earlier, he would've wiped out his family with them going that fast. This was even in the coroner's court. Why wasn't Owen's mum listening? My friend seems to think she doesn't want to believe it but the facts speak for themselves. I know she couldn't stop everything going in the paper, but we haven't had no rest bite. Dr Smiths note was full of shit. That's why he relapses, God I was raging. All this experience living with a child with PTSD, I have cried that many tears I could've made an ocean. I feel broken myself with all the fights I'd had with the government. Even Michael doesn't even know all of these fights I have put up, he has just been signing documents and not knowing, just to keep him away from the stress.

His doctor signed him off for three months sick until he got used to his new medication. So I thought I better write to the Manager Director again to ensure Michael's job was safe. I got a lovely reply back, asking if we could meet and discuss Michael. A week passed and I got a call from a nice lady, she asked if I could meet her at Asda, so we named a time. Michael was unaware of this. When I met with her she advised me that Michael's job would always be safe due to attendance and told me they would do the best for Michael.

So phew, that was one less stress sorted. I felt physically and mentally drained.

I lead a normal life with my foster children who are unaware of everything. They are thriving and unaware of all this.

I'm very proud of my daughter Sharma, only one more year to this date and she will qualify as a nurse. I feel guilty that is has been about Michael but I know she will understand that I am trying to fix him. My husband has been kept in the dark as I have protected them all from my and Michael's hell.

The court case should be over by February 19th, thank God. I wouldn't have to fight PIP or IIDB again until 2020, so I was looking forward to a better 2019.

Michael will carry this PTSD for the rest of his life

but hopefully his anxiety and triggers will be fewer and further between and he can live as normal a life as possible.

The reason for my story is people need to be aware that it is not just soldiers who suffer with PTSD and that it can affect anyone and their families. For me I was the wall trying to protect my family.

So PTSD, you are not destroying my whole family. You have Michael and a bit of me. But I am a fighter and it stops here at me! We will beat you. I have the love from my family and foster children and my amazing best friends, Jackie, Diane, Marion and my counsellor Keith.

If this story helps just one person it is worth telling you all about my hell and my thoughts. So my advice to every one of you is, never give up, stay strong you are never alone and as for benefits, - fight, fight, fight - until you get what you are entitled to!

No one will ever assess my son again if I can help it! They have all the information they need.

There was the possibility that Michael would have to take medication for the rest of his life, but that was a small price to pay to get my precious boy back.

The psychiatrist advised that Michael should take counselling to help get his self-esteem back and to not talk about the accident.

The strange thing was that the therapist then rang me and they thought it was okay to talk about the accident. But I advised them that this was not the case. So it was then put on hold along with the counselling needed to gather more information. He would never talk about it again unless he wanted to. It was up to him. I spent many days talking to Michael about this decision with him in tears.

"I've talked about it for four years. I just want it to end. It's going to be with me forever. I just want to stop talking about it," Michael said.

I agreed with him.

Our life had changed we will always do what we can to protect Michael. Fight, fight, fight, until the day I die.

If anybody is out there that has actually recovered fully from PTSD, I would like to know if this can happen.

I'm going to end this chapter with a poem...

THE PARASITE IN MY HEAD

You took over my head.
Sometimes I think I would be better off dead.
With flash backs, night terrors, panic attacks
and anxiety too,
My mind's that crazy, I don't know what to do.
So when you see me laughing, smiling and full of joy
and think that I am well,
Just look into my eyes, I'm in a living hell.
So please think of others with this parasite living
in their head,
There is no escape, not even in bed.
As all these thoughts run through my head,
Sometimes I think, can I ever recover?
Because living with PTSD is a real motherfucker.

CHAPTER 12
CHRISTMAS 2018

During November 2018, with Christmas just around the corner, I started to see another change in Michael. He was beginning to deteriorate again. It was always the same around Christmas, Mother's Day and the anniversary of the accident.

This time though, it was different. He seemed sad, very sad and was getting verbally aggressive towards me, shouting and swearing in my face. I kept getting the same response every time from him, that he hated himself. And once again I kept it from my family and just between Michael and me. I didn't want my family to worry.

I could also see a bit of a strain in the relationship. Larissa wanted him to give up his flat to be a proper family, but he needed somewhere to escape to when he was feeling low. I felt as if he was giving up and he didn't want any help as he felt as if he was being let down again.

In one of the psychiatrist reports it says he could do with some counselling to build up his self-esteem, and that he should not talk about the accident, which we all thought was a good idea. The defendants agreed and it was all falling into place, until that stupid defendants' doctor wrote his report without even seeing Michael and said it was all caused because of his girlfriend cheating on him!

The defendants had then changed their minds and pulled the counselling from under Michael's feet. That insurance company was the scum of the earth! They are all for taking money for motor insurance, but when it comes to paying anything out, Jesus it's like getting blood out of a stone.

I believe in karma, so that doctor with no shit will get it back tenfold. It's not about the money to me, it's about security. I want to know that Michael will be okay and will always have a home. I want him to get enough to be able to get even a little flat.

Michael's ex-girlfriend had even written to the solicitor explaining how happy and in love they were, they were engaged and planning their lives together. After the accident though, oh, how Michael had changed. He wasn't the man she fell in love with. They tried to be together but he kept pushing her away until she couldn't take it any longer.

I thanked her for writing the letter as she didn't have to and she started telling me little stories about her and Michael. How he used to be the life and soul of the party, the joker, the funny one. I just hoped I would get that Michael back one day…

If it doesn't rain it pisses it down, in our hell.

I couldn't believe the court dates were getting changed. They were supposed to be January 2019 but the solicitor had to get more information about the changes. Bless her she does work hard. I'd cried to her a few times on the phone, I just need someone to listen to me. I bet she thinks I am crazy, but I do thank her for all she does for us.

I just felt sick inside knowing that we were not going to get closure again, and I knew what that meant. More meetings and more assessments!

The new dates were between May and December 2019. I emailed asking her if she could try and get the dates brought forward to as soon as possible as I didn't think Michael could cope with another year of meetings and assessments? Would it push him over the edge if we had to keep doing them? I really hoped the judge took the defendants to the cleaners for putting us through this for the last five years. I was physically and mentally exhausted.

Michael managed to go back to work for a weekend. But he had then been put on sick again for another three months. I actually thought that going to Asda was a trigger for his anxiety as it usually worsened when he had to go to work.

I had spoken to him about leaving and trying to find another job. His response was "Who would want me? I am messed in the head."

Michael hadn't got any friends out of work anymore because he became a recluse and stopped trying.

Michael had told me for some time now he had wanted a phoenix tattoo, but he has now wanted to add a clock to it with the date and birth of his son on it. So I thought right I will pay for it for Christmas for him as a surprise.

So I went to the tattoo shop, spoke to the gu and explained what my son wanted. He said leave it with him and he would design one. The tattoo guy rang me the next day to go and see what he had drawn. I took a picture of it, paid the deposit and booked Michael in for December 28th. I thought I would put the picture in an envelope and give it to Michael on Christmas Day. I thanked the man for his help and left.

As Christmas drew nearer Michael was getting worse. His medication had been upped and I kept telling him there was nothing he could have done on 'that day' and he did nothing wrong. I also told him that he had a nice little family now and to enjoy Christmas.

He then said, "If only."

I stopped him there and said, "You can't live with if only."

I told him it happened and there was nothing he could have done. As for Owen's mum being lonely she had actually met someone else, so she wouldn't be on her own. That I admit was a little white lie but I would say anything to try and make him feel better.

When he was down I got an awful sadness myself and my heart hurt that I couldn't make him better.

Michael said it broke his heart to know how it has affected me. Then when he verbally abuses me I know it's not the real him cause he would never talk to me like that before the accident but it still cuts deep. He always apologies afterwards but it is already planted in my head as I hold my tears back. Michael and Larissa seem a bit all over the place with his depression and anxiety. All I can think about is he has to pull himself together for his kids, Christmas has to be normal for them.

My foster children are oblivious to everything. They don't even know there was an accident. That's how well I have split myself in two - a happy me and a broken me. The broken one is the one no one sees. My children have Christmas Day with their mum and family, which they love and it means more presents, bless them.

The weekend before Christmas Day, Michael was at his worse. He had gone to his flat and no one had seen him. Larissa had spoken to him, but he wouldn't answer the phone to me.

When Christmas was just five days away he locked himself away. The thoughts running through my head were: its Elliot's first Christmas. The girls love Michael and will wonder where he is, he needs to pull himself together for them and put a smile on his face.

Oh my God, why aren't things getting better? My mind was overthinking, praying he would be there on Christmas day, hoping he was there even just for the kids. I couldn't sleep with worry.

Happily, when the weekend was over, he was back with a painted smile, phew! Let's get Christmas out of the way. I had ten people coming over, there was a busy day ahead.

Michael and Larissa and the kids all turned up at 1 o'clock. Michael looked tired but at least he was there. The Christmas meal went without a hitch and everyone left by 7pm and my little darlings were home at 8pm with bags and bags of presents, excitedly telling me about their day and all the chocolates they'd eaten. They'd had an amazing time. At 9.30pm it was time for bed and I knew they would go straight to sleep after the crazy day they'd had.

They all slept in on Boxing Day and when they got up you couldn't see the living room after all the presents they'd got out. My husband's cousin invited us there for snacks and board game night. Michael and Larissa had other plans, but we all went and what a great time we all had. Even though nobody wanted me in their team during the games, apart from Sharma who took pity on me bless her. Even my own husband didn't want me. I don't do well answering questions under pressure. I felt like the child in the playground that no one picks. I was so happy Sharma was home for Christmas, she came back on Christmas Eve with her partner Scott. She was home until January 20th and then had to go back to Scotland for her exams, She qualifies as a disability nurse this year. She is amazing and I couldn't be more proud of her, I love her infinity. Scott could only stay a couple of days as he had to get back for work. We missed him when he'd gone, but what a fantastic night we all had.

The children are playing games in one area, and the adults are playing in another area. My husband is so competitive and hates to lose and our daughter wouldn't give him an inch. It was getting late so I decided to take the kids home, it was 11pm when we left. My husband, Sharma and Scott stayed as my hubby was on a winning streak.

The next morning we all slept in again. It was now December 27th and I rang Michael to remind him that the following day I was taking him to the tattoo studio. Michael was booked in for the ink on that day and he had a two-hour slot in case he wanted to change the design.

He replied, 'Okay, see you tomorrow,' and he sounded fine.

We had a lazy day that day, relaxing and recovering

THE RIPPLE EFFECT

from the Christmas festivities...

On December 28th, I got up and rang Michael to tell him I was on my way round. He didn't sound very chirpy. I soon got to his girlfriend's house, as she only lives two minutes away from me. Michael was still in his pyjamas in the kitchen making a bottle for Elliot.

I asked, "Why aren't you ready? We have to be there in ten minutes."

He replied it won't take me long to get ready and Larissa is upstairs getting ready, so I decided to give Elliot his bottle to give Michael more time to get ready. He came down and he was in a total different attitude and told me I aren't getting it done today, I'll just speak to the guy. I told him I had booked a two-hour sitting so they can discuss it and start. He then proceeded to talk to me like shit, told me he wasn't getting it done, he didn't care about the deposit and gave me a bit of verbal abuse then he went back upstairs and Larissa then came down for Elliot.

I then left the house holding back my tears. I went out of my way doing a nice gesture and he had thrown it all back by verbally abusing me.

When I returned home my husband asked me why I was back so early? I went upstairs and I broke down, why is he like that to me. I do everything for him.

When I get upset in front of Michael he then says I am making it about me.

Is he crazy? Well yeah, actually he is. But he is my son who is broken of course and this affects me.

Can you love your kids too much?

I had hidden my tears for too long. Now my husband

and daughter were seeing it at first-hand. I felt so guilty. My daughter was at home visiting. She should have been enjoying the Christmas holiday, not seeing me like this. But I couldn't hold it back. As the snot ran down my face, something clicked in my head. That was it. I didn't want to see or speak to Michael again until I was stronger. I needed to speak to someone. I needed to share my burden with someone who was not in my family.

That same night I got an apology, but this time I meant business. I told him that he couldn't treat me like that and that I wasn't just going to let it go because he said, 'Sorry'.

Sorry means nothing if you keep doing the damage. I sent a message back saying please don't contact me, my nerves are shattered. I've Sharma and the children to think about and I needed to give them the better side of me. I hadn't seen or spoken to him since December 28th. I felt very guilty but I was no good for him at that time.

On December 29th 2018, two males committed suicide by jumping off the Humber Bridge within minutes of each other. One of them was my daughter's friend. I used to work with his mum Janet. My heart went out to her and her family. Sharma was devastated.

There is really no help for mental health, especially when it comes to benefits. No one really gives a shit. The government is all talk, talk, talk, with no support!

I knew this first hand, it was all about assessments…

CHAPTER 13
HAPPY BIRTHDAY

On January 10th 2019, it was Michael's 30th birthday. We were all going out for tea and I had ordered him a cake for the restaurant to bring out to him. But after the way he'd treated me on December 28th, I cancelled it and sent him £20 for a takeaway and sent his cake for the kids so they could sing 'Happy birthday' to him. I still didn't want any contact with him, as he'd broken me.

I controlled Michael's money so I could ensure his bills were paid and there was a second account, which was just for bills. It had been a while since I had checked his account, so on January 6th I decided to check it to make sure things were up to date.

I couldn't believe it! His account was empty! Had someone stolen his money? He didn't even have a card for his account. But just short of £500 had disappeared. Where had it gone? I had to go straight to the bank and because it was a joint account, they printed me off a statement.

He had spent it!

Michael had been taking money out of it since November and there was nothing left for his bills.

Sharma texted Michael, "You have really done it this time. There's no money for your bills."

He replied, "I fucked up again, I hate myself."

I was so angry as I knew it had probably gone on cannabis as he thinks it's the only thing that helps. Like fuck it does. He only does it when he's bad and goes to his flat, it helps him sleep, calms him down he says. I just think it's in his head now. I don't think it's helping him at all. That's why I wanted Russell Brand to help me to show him he doesn't need it.

So I reckoned that just under £500 had literally gone up in smoke...

After the two poor lads committed suicide a lot of numbers came up on Facebook for mental health lines. I screenshot them to Michael so he could ring them and not me. I was still so angry with him. I still couldn't talk to him but for his birthday I put £200 into his bills account.

I had gone to a support centre to find out if there are any support groups for parents with children with mental health and there was one called 'Rethink'. It was once a month, so I planned to go, it turned out to be on Michael's birthday. So I texted Larissa and said, "I'll beep my horn and I will pass you over the cake and cards." I informed her I would only be two minutes. But when I got there, I beeped my horn and who came walking to the car? Michael!

I felt sick, there he was, walking up to the car. I took a deep breath, got out the car and passed him the cake and cards. He opened his arms to give me a hug, but I couldn't. I just jumped back into my car.

He said, "Is that it?"

I just replied, "Yes," and drove off as I was going to

my first meeting at Rethink.

I had to pull up at the side of the road and text Larissa, "The point of me texting you was because I didn't want to see or speak to Michael."

She responded to my message, "I think Michael thought it was the right thing to do."

The guilt hit me like a brick. He was ill and I was not talking to him! God!

I cried in my car, but then managed to pull myself together and went to the support meeting.

There were about fifteen people there. My heart was racing. Why did he have to come to the car? Am I doing the right thing?

I started to cry in the room and I rushed out to the toilet and tried to pull myself together again. I wiped my face with paper towels and after a few minutes, I went back to the room.

Everyone was lovely, I can't tell you what we spoke about, as it was confidential but now I knew I was not alone. It was one of the best things I had done. It had taken some of the weight off my shoulders and I could keep my family out of it.

I also emailed the solicitor to ask them to try and bring the dates forward. I don't think I can wait another year, and only contact me if it is urgent because everything is driving me crazy. Michael will not deal with this, I deal with everything. I need to now start healing. I have never done this before to Michael I am hoping it will push him to get better and fight. I am not sure if it is the right thing to do? I mentioned it to the group at Rethink and they think sometimes you have to pull back and let them help themselves and it will also take pressure off me. God it is good to know it is not just me that feels this way as we all talked about experiences and we all had different reasons. My husband has asked Larissa to come and see him so he can explain to her why I am the way I am. Five years on a rollercoaster would drive anybody scatty.

I think she understands now that my son who I love dearly is still broken and it breaks my heart to see it.

She told my husband that Michael is doing quite well that he is not seeing me. Was I a part of the problem? Does he feel guilty how it had affected me? Because I feel the same way I am more chilled not seeing him. Maybe this is what we both needed, to be apart for a while. Even my friend said I seem more relaxed. Maybe it is good for us both, the only thing I am worried about if I leave it too long is that it could become awkward between us. I do not want that as I love him infinity.

He hasn't received any sick pay from Asda it should have gone into the bank, if it has stopped what do you do? I will ask at Rethink next month. I'm sure somebody will be able to advise me what to do. No point ringing as you will be on the phone forever. There is somebody attending the support group to ensure the carers are getting what they need. I don't see me as a carer I am just his mum trying to get the best for him. No point ringing benefits as you are on the phone over an hour, probably the same for everybody. After speaking with the solicitor and barrister to me he is not going to get nowhere near enough to give him security for the rest of his life, so that's a big disappointment. That makes me angry. It is a million pound company and he's not going to get enough what I wanted for him.

THE RIPPLE EFFECT

Michael's brain was damaged now - what price did you put on that? He never had mental illness before, or anxiety, or panic attacks, or triggers, or night terrors!

We'd never asked for any of those things but that is what we'd got…

CHAPTER 14
IF MY BOOK'S
A SUCCESS

If my story takes off I'd like to help Michael get a little flat and pay for that lovely lady's son's funeral.

Also, I'd open up a support group myself for PTSD and to help people in the situation, that is not always about the person suffering but those around them and that they are suffering as well.

Someone might pick this book up and think, My God, this is me, and if you do please find a support group or someone to talk to, as this takes a lot of the weight off your shoulders and things will not have the ripple effect on your family.

Sharma's friend who has just committed suicide I have message his mum and told her about Rethink and if she needs to speak, shout, cry or scream then there is help. I know this is far too soon for them, as they are still waiting for his body to be found. But I wanted them to know that they are not alone and there is a mixture of us as parents with mentally ill children and partners. I hope in time that they can get all the help they need and try to make sense of it. It has been five years and I am still trying to make sense of it.

After I'd finished writing my book in May, I went to see my publisher and he suggested that I use my son's real name in the book. I had changed some people's names, including Michael's, who I had re-named Harry, to protect them. I wasn't sure how I felt about that or how Michael would feel about it. I'm not even sure that he knows I've written this, because this is about my journey, and my thoughts and feelings, and the fights I've had in order to protect him. But how could I ask him about it when at the moment I was not even speaking to him.

Plus, I have to send a copy to my solicitor before it can come out with the case still ongoing. But I don't see why not, they may not like what I have said. However, freedom of speech and all that. Everything I have said is truthful it has happened and these are my real thoughts. Well I can't ask him yet anyway, as he has gone away with his girlfriend to the northern lights not sure if this was a birthday treat. I messaged Larissa to say have a good time, as the northern lights are quite spiritual I hope Michael gets inner peace. I have heard they are having a lovely time, well I hope so, I only want good things for my boy. Larissa is an amazing, strong and independent woman who is a great mum and I am so thankful she sees the beauty in Michael.

2018 was a crazy year for me and Michael with ups and downs, meetings and assessments and meetings with social services, meetings with schools and they are not always straight forward but that's a different story. All I will say is, if Offsted wanted real reports on social services and schools they should ask 100 independent carers.

I love fostering, it is one of the best things I have

ever done seeing a child grow, become strong, independent and happy. I would recommend it to anybody if you have a spare room, the only downside and it is not just me who thinks like this is the council social services you get that much conflicted information you never know if you are coming or going. You never know where you stand.

As for one of the schools they did something absolutely disgraceful I have no respect for the school and I was shushed and silenced by the school and social services. They did something really wrong and I was told to be quiet to protect the school's reputation. If this information every got out the reports would have a field day and there be an outcry from the public that's in my opinion, but I have been told to remain silent. So now I know what it is like to be silenced. So it is council social services and a council school they all piss in the same pot so ssssh. I'm sure it will be all swept under the carpet. This is why I believe Offsted should consult 100 random and anonymous carers. I am sure they would be surprised with the feedback. I have spoken to a lot of other carers and we will all come up with the same problems. We are told to make the children part of our family but social services make them feel different with the conflicting information.

That's the only drawback to fostering, you never know where you stand. It is a whole different story, but I'd still recommend it.

I rang 'benefits' today to ask if Asda didn't pay sick anymore what did I need to do, 56 minutes I was put on hold for, just to ask one question. I ended up screenshotting my phone to prove this, and after finally speaking to somebody they said Michael may need to be assessed again. However I will need to get a letter from the doctor again, but this shouldn't be a problem.

Also in 2018, one morning in April, my lovely lady Janet, who I looked after for fourteen years, passed away suddenly.

One of my carers was ringing me so I parked up at the side of the road to take the call. The carer told me that my lady had been rushed to hospital but that's all she knew. As I put the phone down it rang again and it was my lady's daughter Sam, who told me that it wasn't looking good and I needed to get to the hospital. I put the phone down and drove to the hospital with tears in my eyes. The journey was a nightmare, every light turned red and it took me forever to get there. When I arrived my lady's husband, Austin, and her daughters, Sam and Louise were waiting for me outside. They told me that it was only the machine that was keeping her alive, and they wouldn't let them turn it off until I'd arrived as Janet had told them I was her best friend.

The doctors took us all into a side room and explained the machine was doing all the work and my lady had actually died. The words didn't sink in and I kept repeating, "Are you sure?" because a few days before I went to see a spiritualist because I wanted to know if Michael would ever get better.

The spiritualist asked me, "Do you look after a lady?" In his words he said she was not going to need carers. I looked at him surprised and said, "Why, is she going to die?" And he replied, "No, she may need to go into a care home.

I remember saying to the doctor "She can't be dead, the spiritualist told me she wasn't going to die."

They all just looked at me and must have thought I was stupid as tears filled my eyes.

The doctor said to us, "Do you want to come with me whilst I take the tubes out?"

Not for one minute did I think they meant take it from her throat. Oh my God, I didn't realise how big that tube was. I could actually see it moving up her neck and through her throat until it splattered blood from her mouth. I looked at the poor girl's faces.

The shock of it! I was not happy about that, but Austin said that it was his fault for saying we would be there as we all thought it would be just the tubes from her arms.

We all kissed her on her head and said our goodbyes. I can't believe it. Austin said she only went to the toilet and she had a heart attack on the toilet, but the doctor said that was not unusual.

It hit me harder than I thought. The poor girls.

They all kept me involved with the funeral arrangements. Sam says I am her second mum as she was only a young girl when I started there. The lady only had limited speech but I could always understand what she was saying. She even used to make me tell her husband off cause all she could say was fuck off to him. Austin used to say to me it was like having two wives. I had a jumper from my lady so I got two rag dolls made filled with her jumper with a note saying I will always be with you for the girls for Christmas, they received these on Christmas Day 2018.

I think of my lady quite often, she was like Marmite

you either loved her or hated her as she could be quite hot-headed and she could say all the swear words. I and she had an understanding and the carers used to ring me up if she had been having a go at them and she would then always say sorry. My lady trusted me she would never do anything her husband said unless she asked me first and I would then say yeah it's okay and she would then laugh. We will meet again and you're buying.

I miss you Janet.

God bless you until we meet again.

Rest in peace. xxxx.

I think Michael was having a good week but that week was all for Janet...

CHAPTER 15
HOPING FOR
A BETTER YEAR

In early 2019 I started working as a volunteer in a hairdressers on a Friday. In return they pampered me and we all got our hair done for free. I washed hair, answered the phone, swept the floor, made the drinks but my biggest role was to make the customers laugh.

It was the perfect job! I'm a great talker, I can talk for England. My husband always says I never stop talking when I get in, "What the hell do you find to talk about?"

My reply is, "It's good to talk."

I hoped 2019 would be a better year even though we still had a court case hanging around our necks and we'd not be free of closure for another year although I hoped it would be sooner rather than later.

I was still looking after my little autistic boy on a Sunday. I'd been looking after him since he was seven, and he was now eleven and huge. Oh, how time flies.

I look back now and think how the hell did I cope with all that was going on and be normal with my family, with a million and one thoughts going through my head?

I feel as if I lived two lives, one to protect my little family and a second one to fight for Michael and protect him on his roller-coaster ride.

THE RIPPLE EFFECT

It is coming to the end of January and my daughter is going back to Scotland as she has an exam. God, I'm going to miss her so much. I won't see her again until August when we are all going up to Scotland for a little holiday away in a cottage. I love Scotland it is a beautiful place and there government is a lot better than ours. Even though I have good and happy days, I still have the pain of sadness inside that won't shift. I think it's my last son, he's not the son I gave birth too. Will he ever come back? Someone said to me once, that he was alive and I should be grateful that he didn't die. My reply was "No he didn't die, but I watched him mentally tortured daily and maybe for the rest of his life. But is that really living? Imagine your child who you love daily all of a sudden starting to hit himself in his face, pulling his face, hating himself, not washing, the triggers, the flashbacks and the anxiety"

Oh yeah, that was really living! Stupid woman!

Was I the only woman who would feel like that if their son was destroyed mentally? Was there a right or wrong way to be?

Was there a manual to help me?

I never knew if I was doing right or wrong...

In February 2019 I went away again with my friend Jackie. I'd done this for the last three years. Just her and me, relaxing in the sun, recharging our batteries. All we do is sleep.

We're both really boring, neither of us drinks, we go back up to the room and watch a late-night movie with a cup of tea. You would think we were pensioners.

My husband also goes away for a week on a separate,

walking holiday. We don't like to both leave the children at the same time, so we go on a separate one first and then a big summer holiday all together. Last year in 2018 there was eleven of us. We all went to Bulgaria for two weeks and we were knackered when we got back. All of the routines went out of the window with all the late nights. I think I needed another holiday to recover from that one…

Michael and Larissa were at home now but I still hadn't spoken to Michael. I didn't know how to ask him about using his real name in the book, I don't even think he knew about me writing it. I worried that if I did use his name, he might think people were pointing and looking at him. But I'd done this not only for me but also for anyone who had a mentally ill family member or friend - and most of all for him.

I kept asking myself when and how to ask him and decided to bring it up at the next meeting at Rethink and see if anybody could give me any advice…

Sharma had been to see Michael to tell him about the book. She said that him and Larissa were really surprised. He'd said, "Yes, You can use my real name," so here goes…

My beautiful son is called Michael. Writing this book has helped me loads, but once again, my poor daughter - I do feel like my whole life revolves around Michael. But this is how it has to be until he's well.

The good news was that he and Larissa are planning for a future, so maybe I should've pulled back a long time ago but who knows. Sharma is leaving tomorrow for Scotland its Scott's gain and my loss. I miss her so much.

I started visiting my other niece Amanda once a week in Market Weighton, I should've done this a while ago but better late than never. I have been having long talks with them and I would like to thank them for listening to me. However once again I do not have an ending, I wish I did so I can move on.

January 22nd 2019 was another funny day. I'd not seen Michael since the day I jumped out of my car and handed him his birthday cards and cake. But today our paths crossed going to school to pick up the kids. I saw him and paused. I thought what do I do? Do I hide? Do I bury my head?

The guilt hit me. How could I ignore my own son? I love him more than life. I took a deep breath. He's my son. I'd had him for over 30 years. I was not letting him go.

I walked up to him and kissed him on the cheek and told him I love you. And he kissed me on my cheek and then I walked on and thought I did the right thing. I didn't want to ignore him to long, if it carried on how we would ever go back. I am very glad that happened.

I blocked him on my phone on December 28th so he couldn't contact me, but Larissa rang me but when I answered the phone it was Michael and asked me if I wanted the curtains from his flat as he was sorting the flat out. Larissa was making him throw things away that he doesn't use, so I am so pleased. Maybe I pulling away is the push he needed, but no matter how hard I try I cannot see the sparkle in his eyes. If you look deep I can still see the sadness? Is he putting on a front?

The song 'Tears of a Clown' came to mind. I don't know anymore. I really hoped this clear-out was a new beginning for him.

I hoped and prayed he'd become the man I always knew he could be. He had a loving little family that he had always wanted now. It was my time to step back and breathe. I still had a lot of what ifs, and I should practice what I preach - you can't live on what ifs.

For the last five years I'd felt as if I had to fight for everything. I had to cry, scream and shout and split myself into two to protect my family.

I was lucky that I had good friends. Jackie, Marian, Dianne, My niece Amie (who pampers me once a week), Amanda, my auntie Sue, Nick and Fay. Poor Jackie and Amie have had me every week for five years, I still go to Amie's for tea one night a week and Jackie comes to mine one night each week for tea, and Marin maybe once a month. I'm sorry for stressing you all out when you see me cry and I'd like to thank Sue, Nick and Fay for reaching out to Michael.

I would also like to thank Sharma's friend Demi for typing the rest of my story. This was the hardest thing I'd done considering I'm dyslexic. This was how it worked: I read it out and Demi typed it, as no one would ever be able to read my notes as they were all back to front and upside down, and there was only me that could read them. So thank you Demi for typing it for me.

My biggest nightmare is that my relationship with Michael is really strained. I do not really recognise him at times but he knows that I will love him to the day I die and will do anything to help him.

Michael, Sharma and my foster children are my life.

I would also like to thank my husband Gerald for your silent words. I know it hurts you to see me trying to keep it together. Thank you for picking me to be your wife. I love you so much.

CHAPTER 16
TOO GOOD
TO BE TRUE!

In the middle of March 2019 we finally received some new court dates for June, which I was so happy about. I much preferred that they were sooner rather than later. I planned not to tell Michael until the night before because then he wouldn't get stressed about it. It was going to be a two-day trial, fingers crossed. We were going to get closure at last and there'd be a new beginning for us all…

Then once again – You're joking! - I knew it was too good to be true!

I received a phone call a week later whilst shopping in Asda saying that the court dates might get changed again. I started crying in the middle of the supermarket as I thought, OMG - we were not going to get closure after all!

It was a good job that my friend Jackie was there, as I must have looked a right idiot as the tears rolled down my face.

Every time I got hope and thought it was going to be over and my boy could start healing, it then all changed. I think they were pulling together a meeting with the barristers - and I'd find out more about that when my solicitor contacted me.

THE RIPPLE EFFECT

Also in that same week I was told that my three beautiful and amazing foster children - that I'd been told more than once were long term and that we'd have them until they were 18 - may be getting returned to their mum.

In my opinion it was to do with council cuts. I was so against it and social services will not be getting my blessing. There was more to this story than met the eye. I felt as if I'd lost my trust with social services. I told them if it all went tits up and the children deteriorated, I would be pointing my finger at them and it would just become another statistic where the social services had let them down.

This really upset me as we'd given the children the best life possible and it showed as they were meeting all their targets and doing amazingly well.

The only thing that made me feel better was that I'd told the social worker she'd be signing for this and she'd be responsible if they ended up back in the system and being passed from carer to carer. But that also scared me as the children would not be able to come back to me. I'd be full again by that time as I'd have the room for another set of siblings, and there was always a shortage of carers for siblings.

I also had a meeting at Rethink and someone from benefits was there and I can't believe it Michael could have claimed five years ago - because he worked on and off, he was entitled to something. A lovely man called Sam has been helping me to sort this out. I told Sam that I did ring five years ago and I was told, 'No.'

We hadn't had anything yet but I wasn't surprised, benefits always seemed to take a long time.

Michael had just been put on sick for another six months. Asda was 100% a trigger as he got ready to go to work he had a massive panic attack, where he thought he was having a heart attack and he got really upset. I don't think he will ever go back.

Larissa said she couldn't even shop there with him as he started to panic. I can't believe nearly five years and I am only finding stuff out from Rethink. I was talking at the meeting about how you want to protect your kids but everyone wants to assess them. It caused a massive impact and it caused them too much stress. Sometimes you do not want to even apply for anything to keep them protected as sometimes it makes things worse. I really could understand why the mentally ill don't claim. It was far too stressful seeing different people all the time. It would drive anyone mad. Why couldn't one report do for everything?

A lady at Rethink told me you can get a letter from your doctor saying that he cannot be assessed due to mental health. So I rang the doctor and Hallelujah - it was true. The doctor wrote a letter and they would process it without seeing him. They would just go through me and would leave Michael alone.

I couldn't believe it. It had only taken me five years to sort that out.

Our doctors' surgery was fantastic. They were so helpful and I had an amazing relationship with the receptionist Sam. In fact all of the staff there were amazing. They were aware of Michael's mental health and they bent over backwards to help me. I was so grateful to them all, thank you.

I still felt a strain between me and Michael and I felt

as if he thought that he was a waste of space. I told him every time I saw him that I loved him and he was amazing and that he was just unwell. He just needed to be strong and we would beat PTSD together.

Knowing he didn't have to go to Asda was helping his recovery. He spent more time with Larissa and the kids, which I was happy about. We took every day as it came and there was no pressure on him to work. You could see how relieved he was. I wish I could have changed the past and not have pushed him to return to work and a 'normal life' too soon. Maybe I should have left him to know when he was ready. I felt guilty for pushing him back to work. Did I really do the right thing trying to give him normality? Or had I actually caused him more anxiety and panic attacks?

Why didn't I know about Rethink sooner as we all talked and they said I was doing the right thing but he needed to do things in his own time and when he felt that he was ready?

It was true that I had seen a change. I was feeling relaxed knowing he was calmer. My only worry was that my three foster children might be getting returned to their mum, even though I had a fantastic relationship with them. I had told their mum how I felt and bless her, she responded saying she didn't expect me to feel any different as she could see how much I loved the kids and how much they loved me.

I still look after Kian, my little autistic boy every Sunday and in the holidays. He was four when I started looking after him, now he's eleven. He can't talk but he has echo syndrome where he can only repeat and he seems to have picked up some naughty words. He kept calling his auntie 'a motherfucker'.

I was trying to teach him not to say it, as it was a naughty word. He even shouted it in Asda and I could've died but he doesn't understand although hopefully other people will. I would love to know where he picked it up from.

My daughter said that if my story was ever made into a drama, then Myra, an actress from Hollyoaks should play me because her character is just like me. Sharma sent me video clips all the time, saying mum this is just like you and I laughed my head off. The worst thing was though, I could see exactly what she meant. But I was maybe getting ahead of myself and nobody would probably care about my book and it would just end up in the bin...

It was that time again and I'd gone away again with my friend Jackie whilst my hubby was at home to recharge. I can't believe how much I slept with a hundred thoughts going through my head. It was already a year ago this month since my lady, Janet, passed away. She often pops into my head and I still see her children Sam and Louise and her husband, Austin.

Sam was only a young girl when I started looking after her mum and had now turned into a beautiful and amazing young lady. Her mum would be very proud of her. I didn't really see much of Louise as she had already left home, but I popped to see Sam a few days ago as it was her birthday and we had a good laugh. I also informed Austin that if he ever needed a carer I was only a phone-call away but he just called me a cheeky sod…

CHAPTER 17
ANOTHER BOMBSHELL

I still hadn't heard from the solicitor about if they were changing the dates or not, I think she was waiting to hear from the judge. But as the saying goes, no news is good news.

When I was away with Jackie I'd met my 'personality twin' called Jill. I can honestly say I'd never laughed so much, she was one crazy lady. It was like watching my husband and me. I had never felt as calm and relaxed in the last five years. I don't normally drink, and it was the first time Jackie and me hadn't gone back to the room to watch a movie as we were having such a good time with our new friends.

The only problem I had whilst I was on holiday was that the solicitor contacted me to ask for my thoughts about if the parties wouldn't pay for more treatment, then the payment might have to come out of Michael's compensation when he finally got it.

Universal Credit wanted more information - the only thing they hadn't got was his blood. I was starting to regret even applying for it. I felt as if it was taking its toll on me.

Why should Michael pay for it out of his compensation? The compensation was important, as it was for his security.

Asda was a trigger, but who else was going to employ him when he had so many triggers.

In my opinion his brain had been damaged with PTSD.

I would him sooner get nothing and for that day never to have happened and for him to live a normal life and not to be fighting with his thoughts.

He told me that he still thinks about it every day. As soon as he wakes up, he says it is there in his mind and he just tries to block it out.

I told the solicitor that I was happy for it to go to court as long as Michael got what he was entitled to, because let's face it, the son I gave birth to had changed and we now lived with it day by day. I just wanted it to be over so we could heal. I was getting tired, so he must be really tired of it all.

He had been put on 'sick' again for six months and he did seem a lot calmer. But he still got so angry. I upset him a couple of times when I flinched as he raised his hands in the air in anger and pulled at his hair.

He said to me, 'Mum, I would never be violent with you.'

I told him that I knew he wouldn't but old habits die hard. I was in a violent relationship from the age of 16 to 22 and those times are hard to forget.

He talked about moving in with Larissa and the children and I thought that was really positive. But he would still need his time out. He said that he just wanted to be normal and to live a normal life…

OMG – the next day the Solicitor got in touch to tell me that the solicitors and the barristers had arranged a meeting for March 25th. This was really positive, maybe they could come to an agreement so there was no court case. This was really good news for me. As you are aware I did not tell Michael anything - I would just tell him what had been decided afterwards. I prayed that it could be settled out of court.

But then more questions! Universal Credit needed more information! They had every single thing, psychiatrist's reports, doctor's reports, wage slips, etc.

I now wished I had really not bothered. They emailed me nearly every week and kept asking me for a meeting. They already had the information and they then kept telling me to ignore the emails. But how could I ignore them when they said that my claim would be void if I didn't respond?

This was constant and was driving me scatty and causing me more anxiety.

I didn't know what else they wanted. I just felt as if I had been fighting for what was right for five years and I couldn't rest until it was over and Michael could be free.

My precious daughter Sharma had followed her dreams and would soon become a nurse. I just couldn't wait to rest my mind and focus on my daughter and for my loving husband that I adore to see me calm. I just wanted to be able to rest my thoughts. So that holiday was the perfect time for me to recharge and Gill and Ray made it extra special. Hopefully we would stay in touch. We were planning to go down to see them for a weekend as soon as we could.

A funny thing happened the following day. I woke up and thought I wonder what the weather is like? And then I realised that I was at home. As soon as I realised I was in my own bed I had a bit of an anxiety attack. I think it was because it was the day the solicitors and the barristers were having a meeting. I was just pleased that Michael didn't have to go. Maybe we would get closure after the meeting and we could be happy as a family because if he had to go through a court case he could spiral out of control.

The saying is you're damned if you do and damned if you don't. This Universal Credit malarkey was more trouble than it was worth. It was really getting on my tit. A week had gone and I still had not heard from the solicitor, but to me no news was good news. Michael seemed okay. I knew we had a court case maybe hanging over our heads but he didn't know, so he seemed quite happy.

The anniversary of the accident was just around the corner. I was praying that he didn't realise and that it didn't get a lot of publicity again.

My friend asked me what Michael thought about the book? I replied that he hadn't really said much and that he was not bothered about it. But what he had said was that if it helped with my healing then he was pleased I was doing it.

I don't think he realised how much I'd struggled to keep it together and to keep the ripple effect at bay. I told him that when the book came out, not to read it until he was strong enough.

Then another bombshell!

OMG - you couldn't make it up!

The solicitor rang to inform me that the other party hadn't turned up to the meeting as they'd gone into liquidation! It was just not sinking in. I just felt sick to the stomach. OMG - is this real? She then tried to explain what would happen next but don't ask me what she said after that.

How can an insurance company go bankrupt? My mind was racing. Was Michael going to end up with the bill? Was he not going to get his compensation? Were we not going to have an ending? Was this going to carry on for another five years?

She explained the next steps but it was all just a blur. My boy couldn't go through it all again.

I said goodbye to the solicitor, not knowing what she'd said, apart from something about they were going to get it from somewhere else. I put the phone down and just cried.

That night I found it hard to sleep. Then, the first thing I thought about when I woke up was that I couldn't go through it all again. And if I couldn't go through it again, Michael definitely couldn't.

Was I over-thinking everything? Should I tell him or shouldn't I? I couldn't remember what the solicitor said.

I was in shock. I just wanted it all to end. The court case was definitely cancelled. I was in tears. No closure again. I felt as if my brain was going to explode.

The psychiatrist still wanted Michael to have more treatment. I was going to have to tread carefully as I didn't want to rock the boat with his mental health.

I thought all right; he didn't need to know about the insurance company going bankrupt, as that would really stress him out. I thought I'd only tell him about the treatment but I'd speak to Larissa first. I explained everything to her, and she rang back to tell me that he was willing to have the treatment and that she had also told him about the bankruptcy.

Michael then rang me. He was really stressed and said that he couldn't go through it all again and that he couldn't see different people again.

His stress levels were really high. It caused a bit of a fall out between Larissa and me but she thought that he had a right to know everything.

But who was right?

I guessed that we just had to disagree on that one.

Again I couldn't sleep. Who was going to pay the solicitor's bills now?

I told the people's manager at Asda what had happened and he said, 'God! You couldn't write this.'

He's a lovely young man and is very helpful, even though sometimes I think I might 'do his head in'.

To be fair Asda as a company had been very good, although I still hadn't spoken to the store manager since the meeting, which was now a long, long time ago…

CHAPTER 18
A LIFE IN LIMBO

In May 2019 we celebrated my grandson's first birthday. He's really clever and was already walking and talking. I don't really speak about this as I keep my joy and my happiness with him separate.

Michael is an amazing dad, not only to his son, but also to the two girls. The baby is definitely a 'daddy's boy' and I see the light in Michael's eyes and the smile on his face when he talks about him and the girls.

Maybe one day he will understand how his illness has affected me, because when we've cried he sometimes said, 'But mum, it happened to me,' and he doesn't understand why I was crying.

And I say, "I know it did, but you are my son and when you're hurting, I'm hurting.'

So this ending could be years away, as there was still no ending in sight.

I would like to thank two more friends Claire and Leanne for listening to me. I still work at the hairdressers on a Friday. I help out and make the customers laugh and it makes me feel normal. I am lucky to have good neighbours including Maria and Chris. Maria always invites us to their BBQs but she keeps reminding me she owes me a payback from years ago. I won't be surprised if she gets Ant and Dec involved, even though I think it was her own fault. It was her birthday and I bought her a scratch card and put 5p in the card so she could scratch it. I asked a couple of times at the party had she done it and she said, 'I'll do it later.'

Her and her husband got me drunk so I went home and straight to bed. This was before we had the foster children.

The first thing I thought when I opened my eyes was, shit, the scratch card! I thought I'd better go and ring her to see if she'd done it. But it was too late - she had already done it! She had already left a message on my phone. You see it was a fake scratch card.

She'd got up at 5am to get a drink of water and decided to do her scratch card. She thought she'd won a hundred thousand pounds. She then woke the full house up to tell them that they were rich. All the family sat around her whilst she tried to ring everybody that she knew. That's when she realised the card was fake and all that I can say is that the phone call she made to me wasn't very nice, But we laugh about it all the time now and she always says revenge is sweet and she is waiting to have hers. I'm sure she's waiting until my 50th to do something. I'll have to be on my guide…

At the time, I had my daughter's friend Demi staying with us. She'd spilt up with her boyfriend so she was staying with us for a few days. I just kept winding her up and she just laughed. The foster children loved her being here and so did I.

Then it was the countdown to Sharma coming home

in two weeks time. I couldn't wait to give her hugs and kisses, I really missed her. Scott couldn't now come due to work commitments and I'd miss the Scottish twat. Only joking, I love you really Scott…

So I think this is the ending - as least as far as the ending can go.

What have I learnt?

There's no help for PTSD sufferers unless you're in the army.

Mental health affects the whole family not just the person who suffered the trauma. And even though the NHS do their best it's not enough as they are over-stretched and underpaid which meant we got no help.

Trying to sort out benefits has been hell - it's an absolute joke.

Universal Credit, the left hand doesn't know what the right hand is doing. I just got asked for the same information all the time, for things they already had. I feel sorry for the homeless and the mentally ill who have nobody to help them. That's probably why they go begging in the street. At one point I was tempted to go on the street myself, that's how unbelievable it is.

Never believe what you're told from social services as they always give you constant conflicting information and they change it so many times.

The kids don't even know where they stand because every social worker has different ideas and change things all the time. I've seen this first hand. It's crazy but true!

Some schools only want to protect their reputation and it is all about the grades. Again, I have witnessed this at first hand. They don't have to pretend they really care, I know and they know what they did but we have to protect the school's image.

What a load of shit!

Oops! Sorry, Ssshh! I'm not allowed to talk about it.

I know I may sound negative about a lot of things but this is how it's been in my experience, so the positives won't take very long to list…

1. The Doctors surgery has been amazing their help and support they have shown me has been unbelievable. I would like to thank you all as you have seen me at my worst, for your kind words and for listening to me. I will always be grateful.

2. Asda the company I am very grateful for and for Andrew the peoples manager and not forgetting Shirley the till manager you stood by Michael and helped as much as can. Shirley you helped Michael during meltdowns I don't think you realised how much you helped him. You're a blessing in disguise.

3. To all my friends you know who you are you have listened to me sobbing as I have tried to get help.

4. My daughter Sharma, who I seem to have neglected for five years. I'm so proud of you and love you dearest. And Scott, thank you for looking after her.

5. My beautiful foster children, you keep me busy and our house full of laughter. We share our love with each other. And an even bigger positive is that the children were staying put. Mum told me that the Social workers took three weeks to tell me that.

6. To my husband who doesn't say much but supports me through everything. He has never really known the full impact, as I will not let the ripple pass me. Thank you for picking me to be your wife.

7. To Larissa, thank you for loving Michael and for giving him a loving son and a lovely little family, even though I know sometimes things can be hard.

8. Last is Michael. The devil had destroyed your life and the evil parasite, PTSD had taken over your mind. I know we are still fighting everyone and everything but never give up hope. We will fight this demon together. I love you. You, Sharma and all the children are my sunshine in morning and my starts at night and one day this torture will end and we will have closure once and for all. But who knows. Never give up hope and if my story takes off I will pay for Michael to go to a private clinic in America to help fight this and make him realise he doesn't need cannabis to help him relax. I will keep my word to the lady and help to pay for her son's funeral. I would open a group for PTSD sufferers, not just for people in the services.

In May 2019, it was the fifth anniversary of 'that day' and I knew what was coming. Michael would deteriorate and we would go through a bad time for a while. I couldn't believe it - nearly five years and still no closure, no help and no compensation. And was it going to court? Your guess was as good as mine.

We still had no ending and we were just stuck in limbo. If anybody could see the life sucked out of your child that was how it felt. He couldn't socialise with people because of the anxiety, panic attacks, triggers, anger and sadness - that was his life.

I've been reading back my story and I can't believe how angry and crazy I've sounded. I'm so glad I started at the support group to put things into perspective. What happened to my son makes my heart ache. And when people say, "Yes, but at least he lived," I think, but can you really say what he's going through is living?

What had those five years done to me?

Well, I can tell you one thing they'd done to me - I'd put on over two stones!

I comfort eat. I eat when I'm sad, anxious, stressed, angry and worried. I used to look like a large, juicy pear but now I look like a big, fat jacket potato. In fact, two big, fat jacket potatoes, as one is just my head. If this goes on for another five years I'm going to look like a pumpkin. Everyone knows how hard it is to lose weight once you've gained it. Even my boobs have gone from a DD to an F. I've been trying to squeeze these F boobs into a DD bra. Instead of looking down and seeing two lovely coconuts I now look down and see two babies' heads. If it carries on for another ten years they will need to get a crane to lift me off the couch. The only time I don't comfort eat is when I'm happy.

OMG!

Am I ever going to lose this weight and get the twins out my bra and go back to the coconuts?

I'll tell you when its over. Then this fat lady will be singing...

CHAPTER 19

WILL THE NIGHTMARE EVER END?

Someone call the bank manager!

Michael got paid by Universal Credit - £50 and £8 wages from Asda. Wow all this money! What bills should I pay first?

On a serious note though, I needed to ring Asda. I 'd tried the manager who looked after Michael but he must have been having a day off, so I'd try again on Monday.

Yes I was right, the Asda manager was on holiday so I spoke to someone else and asked why Michael hadn't been paid any sick pay. They said they think it might be because it's a new tax year and that he should get it in next month's wages. I have seen Michael a few times and he seems to be up and down. He hates the fact he can only ring me on the house phone rather than my mobile as this is a part of my recovery. Because every time his name comes up on my phone I get the feeling of anxiety and a feeling of dread because that is how it has been for the last five years. When he rang in the past he had always been crying and in a state because of his PTSD. I am not used to a normal call from him anymore to say, "Hi mum, are you alright?"

I just normally get stressed calls and angry calls and it does affect me greatly. If he needed me in an emergency he could contact through his dad's phone or the house phone and this had really helped my recovery from no contact through my mobile. In the past he always knew he could never ring me twice as my heart would start racing and it would really stress me out. I had told him that if I didn't answer it was probably because I was driving and that I would ring him right back. When I do eventually call him back he is usually crying and my heart shatters into a thousand pieces. I can't get through to him and it kills me inside. I find myself talking about everyday stuff just to get him to calm down. I cannot believe we are just weeks away from five years and nothing has really changed, apart from the insurance company going bankrupt and that's all gone tits up.

God only knows what was going to happen now? I know that they say money doesn't buy you happiness but it does give you security and peace of mind knowing that your bills and rent will be paid.

But would he ever return to work? Would anyone employ him now with all these triggers?

I had to contact the solicitor to find out if the CBT treatment was still going ahead and who was going to pay for it. I knew that the solicitor said something along the lines that the government insurance should be okay but that they might have to contact them. But when I talked to the solicitor nothing sank in - it was all a blur. I would have to just wait and see.

I could see a strain again in Michael's relationship. I am a bit gutted as Larissa is really good for him and she is a strong minded and fantastic mum but even I know how hard it is when Michael got stressed with all the thoughts going through his head.

He really does need this next lot of treatment. We are just waiting to see who is going to pay for it. I'd like to say it's hard to believe that we're nearly five years on and nothing has been decided. But it's not!

Will the nightmare ever end? Or was it going to be a long and never-ending waiting game?

Like the psychiatrist said, Michael could never start his full recovery until we'd got some kind of closure. Did that mean he was going to have to depend on benefits for the rest of his life? I really hoped not as he'd always worked since leaving school. And it was unbelievable how one horrific afternoon, five years ago, could change a life, maybe forever.

I knew he depended on cannabis and I know I have mentioned Russell Brand a few times but that was only because I'd watched a programme where he'd helped drug users come clean. I really hoped that he saw my story and helped me to get my lost boy back.

Don't get me wrong we do have good days and his son Elliot is the light of his life. I can see the sparkle in his eyes when he speaks to me about him but we still get the dark times when the devil PTSD takes over. So if anyone has suffered from PTSD and then totally recovered from it, I'd love to hear from them...

During May the only thing I wished for was that I could close my eyes and it would be June, as I knew what was coming - the storm in Michael's mind.

Good days are precious to me now, they are the days I don't have to worry about PTSD and the ripple effect. It had put us both through a living hell and had also helped me to realise how powerful your brain is.

I wished that there could be a magical hypnotist who could make Michael forget the trauma. Can you imagine how many millions of people that would help?

To be able to wipe thoughts from your memory. All the people that suffer with tortured minds, not to remember your bad past and then your mind can be at peace. No more fighting the devil. If only that was possible…

Some say that it's good to talk and get it out. But in Michael's case it made it worse. So maybe for him, locking it in a box and never speaking about it again would be the best thing to do. Who knows, as there is not enough support? Everyone these days is overworked and underpaid and everywhere is understaffed and bursting at the seams and we are just the minions plodding along.

Since the day of the accident we'd had a beginning but not an ending. I know the day will come but will my boy ever be the same? I only hope he makes peace with his mind.

Whilst Sharma was at home she paid for her dad and me to go glamping for two nights. Can I just say we laughed for two nights - we took vodka and brandy and we do not drink - but we ended up as drunk as skunks and were the only ones on the campsite. My husband said we'd have to turn the music down at 10 o'clock to respect our neighbours. The silly sod - we were the only ones there. I said, "What neighbours - the invisible ones?"

THE RIPPLE EFFECT

We did suffer in the morning it didn't take us a lot to get drunk. We had a fantastic time only to come home to find another letter from Universal Credit stating they wanted Michael to have another medical assessment.

OMG - are they crazy? They had everything. It was getting beyond a joke and I was sick of it. I rang and told them that if they gave him another assessment it could push him over the edge.

I also told them, although I shouldn't really have said it, that I'd burn their building down. I did apologise when I'd calmed down and told them I would sooner him get nothing than have another assessment.

Plus it was coming to the anniversary of 'that day'.

I left a message with Sam who works for Universal Credit and he told me if we didn't show up for the medical twice then Universal Credit would make the decision.

Is there any wonder that we have all these suicides?

An assessor cannot look inside your head. I was fuming. I'd just come home from a stress-free two days but within a few hours was already stressed again. What a shambles it all was!

Yes, he could bend. Yes, he could stand. Yes, he could touch his head and his toes. And yes, he could stand and he could talk! But he couldn't fight the fucking demons in his head!

They'd got doctors' letters and psychiatrist's reports stating that assessing him again could do more harm to his mental health. Yet they decided they still wanted to assess him! They needed their heads testing. I'd hold them responsible if they went ahead and it pushed my boy over the edge.

I was fuming. They told me they'd ring me back within 24 hours. They wanted to do the assessment on May 16th - just over a week before the anniversary of the accident!

It was not happening! Even if I had to go on my own and take everything with me, they were not messing with his head! He was already starting to get on edge.

I waited for the assessment team to ring me, then unbelievably someone from Universal Credit said they would be ringing Michael regarding a job search, and helping him get back to work!

Were they sick in the head?

He'd got a job but he was on sick. He was waiting for treatment to build up his confidence and control his stress levels and his anger and try to hopefully get him some control back, as when he went back to work he had an anxiety attack! The way he was being treated you'd think that he'd been on benefits all his life! It was his first time. Why did I ever bother?

I asked to speak to somebody higher up but no one passed the information on. My mind just kept going over and over it. I thought I might even get in touch with my MP Karl Turner to see if he could do anything.

I don't tell Michael anything because it gets me down as I fight to protect 'my lost boy'.

'Reach' by S Club 7 is my song for Michael, as he needs to leave the past behind him and follow his dreams. When I hear that song I get goose bumps and I start singing it really loudly as if I'm singing it to him, as I will always be there for him.

When I think of Owen who lost his life I can't help but think I also lost my boy that day. I hope Owen's mum can understand how it has been for both of us in different ways. I honestly believe Michael will never be the same and we will be fighting every day that comes. But I know that I have to never give up hope...

CHAPTER 20

FIGHTING FOR BENEFITS

Trying to get benefits has been an absolute nightmare and it's still not sorted. Mental health - we can't see it - but we live with it. It's a constant struggle. I wrap Michael in cotton wool and never tell him what happens in the background as the simplest of things stress him out.

Five years ago he was never like this - nothing ever bothered him. He was always happy, the joker, the clown. He always thought all the girls fancied him and now he is just an empty shell. I've looked after foster children now for over nine years, but never did I think I'd lose my own child to PTSD. But it can happen to anybody - women, men, girls, and boys - anybody - not just soldiers. And in my opinion the government are just letting people down who suffer with PTSD. They need to put more money into the NHS and lower the government's bonuses. We, the people, should have priority over the big, fat political cats who fill up their pockets.

Sharma had just been home for the Easter holidays and was heading back to Scotland for her final exam before becoming a nurse. I loved spending time with her, we're so alike and the kids loved her being at home.

THE RIPPLE EFFECT

I had a full house of seven of us at times and I often forgot how hard it was to cook for that many. And sometimes there were the three grandkids and Kian, the little autistic boy here as well, which made it eleven people.

Some might say I live in a mad house. I just say it keeps me sane. If I was kept busy I couldn't think of other things. I know that even Kian's mum had to fight to get help for her little boy and he sometimes gets frustrated and trashes up the house. But he can't talk so you can never really find out what is really troubling him. But when he is at mine he laughs most of the day. I think that's because there are other kids in the house. In fact, I was blessed with my three foster children because they fitted into my family like a glove. They were so happy and they talked really highly about us to the social workers. The youngest always talked about my food and cooking and how good it is. And the other two always talked about all the activities that we do. We also have a fantastic relationship with their parents. It's unusual for foster parents and parents to get on, but it works for us and everything fits. I would still recommend fostering if you have a spare room. It's the best thing we have ever done. Even though I don't always agree with the social workers and in my opinion sometimes they totally get it wrong.

But as my husband says, "They're overworked and underpaid and have a massive work load, so sometimes they are going to get it wrong."

I think I'm a strong woman and will always fight for what is right for anyone and if they make a mistake I am always the first one to point it out and speak my mind.

I think I come across sometimes as being aggressive but it is just that I'm passionate and I want what is best for them. The school and social services let one of them down massively but I won't go into that. That secret is safe.

The following week I went to Scotland with Sharma for a few days to catch up with Scott and his parents whilst my husband was off work. I will not see Sharma again until September. I tell her all the time that she's a beautiful, kind, caring and a loving woman who deserves to be happy in whatever she does. I really miss her when she's away and I still feel a bit guilty that the five years had just been about trying to get Michael well. But she always says that she understands and tells me not to worry and that he needs me, bless her. I still feel guilty about it though.

Three men in my area had committed suicide since December, which just said it all really. They were the only ones that had been in the paper, but the chances were that there had been more that we hadn't heard about. My heart went out to their families as I'd seen it first hand when your child was fighting with their mind and wanting to be normal - but most of all just wanting to be happy.

Will Michael ever get that peace? I can only hope and pray that he will, but only time will tell. I just want this month to be over. I had a cry in the park this morning, Universal Credit is driving me crazy. I rang the assessment team to explain everything and said someone was supposed to call me back but they never did. The young man on the phone explained that all the information Universal Credit had, had not been passed on to the assessment team. He explained he would transfer me through to the assessors, he was really nice. But as he was putting me through, I got cut off. So I rung back and waited ten minutes and a different man answered the phone and asked me how he could help?

I said OMG - I don't want to go through it all again. I explained that the phone had just been put down on me and the guy who I was talking to was transferring me to the assessors. I said the call would be on the system and that he could transfer me through to the relevant department.

The guy's response was that I'd already wasted a minute and twenty seconds of his time and there were people waiting for a call - and if I didn't explain to him exactly what I wanted, he was going to put the phone down on me.

I had to apologise and then I had to go through the story again. I only apologised so he wouldn't put the phone down on me. But after all that, he still wouldn't transfer me and advised me he would just give me the phone number. At this point I was crying. I spoke to a lovely lady called Charlotte and she told me they hadn't received anything from Universal Credit and they were still waiting for a form from the doctors. She gave me the fax number so I could send her everything. I explained that Michael has severe PTSD and that I hadn't even told Michael about the assessment as it was too close to the anniversary and I didn't want to tip him over the edge. So she said she'd put a hold on that appointment and to send all the documents over to her.

I called Sam back at Universal Credit and explained it all to him and he explained it all to his manager. They then said they'd send the documents over themselves. Poor Sam, bless him, I was in tears. I was sick of it all, it was driving me crazy. He said to just contact him if I needed him. He'd done nothing but show me compassion and I was thankful for that. I couldn't believe that the guy from the Assessment Centre made me cry and normally I would put the phone down on them. But he had me by the balls as I didn't want to be cut off again...

I saw Michael a day later and he was on edge and stressed. He also had a bit of anxiety as it was nearly 'that time' again when the devil took over. I don't think he had any cannabis that day, and I was not giving him money for drugs. Because I'd be dammed if I did and dammed if I didn't. I know he depends on it now.

The problems with benefits were putting my stress levels through the roof. I'm the one who was supposed to be sane and the thing was the benefits weren't even for me. I'd talked to the office manager Sam from Good Heart Surgery and she'd told me she hadn't even received the form. She asked for the details and she was going to ring and get it sorted. They'd gone above and beyond helping me and I'd also got myself an appointment because my hands and feet kept swelling up. But I was that busy that I hadn't had chance to go. But Sharma and Jackie made me go as I didn't realise it could be dangerous. They took my blood pressure and it was through the roof. It was 169/140! I didn't know what that meant but they looked really worried and took a load of bloods. I explained my blood pressure was probably high because of Universal Credit and because someone from the Assessment Centre had made me cry as he was rude to me. Sharma was that angry that she rang and asked for a complaints form. Then Sam from Universal Credit called and advised that everything had been sent and for me to take it easy and try not to be too stressed. I had to go back to the doctors the next day and they sent me home with a blood pressure machine on my arm.

I cannot stress enough how hard it is to get benefits. The way it was going I'd be carried out in a coffin. Could you imagine what it would do to someone who was vulnerable?

The crazy system meant I had to go back to the doctors the next day as well. My blood pressure was through the roof on my first visit but was a lot better on my second. And I knew it was all because of that horrible little man from the Assessment Centre. I was definitely going to complain about him because he showed no compassion for me and we had to go over everything again, about why and what had happened. I just wished I never had to talk about it again.

If the council thought I had STS (Secondary Trauma Syndrome) then surely me having to talk about it every week to Universal Credit was not helping my recovery. Every time I rang I had to explain everything over and over again to the Universal Credit or the Assessment team. This had been going on every week for the last three months. I was so glad I was going to my counselling meetings with Rethink, as they helped me a lot to express my feelings. So for anybody who has mentally ill children or family members, look up your local Rethink because we are all in the same situation and it has really helped me...

CHAPTER 21
WHAT'S ANOTHER YEAR?

In May 2019 I finally got to Scotland to enjoy a break with Sharma. We normally didn't get any time on our own as we usually had a 'house full'. But I remember sitting in the canteen waiting for her to finish her last exam before I took her out for a celebration meal.

In fact I think I could have sat the exam because I'd been helping her to revise, bless her, she always tried her best and always worked so hard. I asked her all the questions and she told me all the answers - we were at it on and off for three days. She definitely did her best and I knew the kids were going to love it having a week in gorgeous Scotland, as it's a beautiful place.

But then, surprise surprise! I had a message again from Universal Credit saying they were not back-paying Michael even though I was told he was not entitled to anything for November, December and January, as he was classed as employed - even though he received no wages.

They told me I could appeal even though I have asked them to reconsider, the only back pay is for special circumstances apparently. But what was more special than being told you were not entitled to anything?

I am not going to appeal, as it is far too stressful. I would sooner get nothing than be stressed. His Dad and me have been paying his bills and keeping him afloat for the last few months. They run me down to my bones. That was what benefits had done to me! Every morning when I woke up I got a rush of dread and my heart started pounding, it was definitely anxiety!

I even got that feeling when I saw an email from Universal Credit or the solicitors, as they were always to do with something for Michael and someone always wanted something. All I ever wanted was for him to receive his compensation so that he didn't have to worry about anything other than getting well. But that was not going to happen any time soon.

I was absolutely gutted that he was having to go on benefits even though it wasn't yet sorted. I just wished he could go back to Asda. I just hoped that the CBT treatment works.

I'd never really understood anxiety until I got it, it's a horrible feeling. It makes you feel really sad and even though I've an amazing little family who I love dearly, the stress is unbelievable. With me having to go over and over it I was never going to get peace, because I had to constantly explain why Michael was not to be assessed. As I've said before, one assessment should do for everything.

I hadn't seen Michael for four days whilst I was in Scotland, but I went to see him as soon as I got back and he was on edge and quite stressed. God knows what he was going to be like in the next thirteen days. He normally started to deteriorate and it was his son's first birthday on May 17th. They were doing him a little garden party and that would keep his mind busy. Michael struggled being around people and I could already see the deterioration in him.

I'd actually forgotten what it was like to wake up and feel normal and good to be alive. Those days had gone. Don't get me wrong, once I was up I was okay, but it was the waking up that was the problem. It was all the harassment and stress from Universal Credit.

When I saw Michael again he was still really stressed and worrying about his bills. He actually said, 'I wanna go back to work but I can't until it's all over. I need my treatment mum. I just want it to be over.'

So I rang the solicitor and they said to go ahead with the CBT treatment and that Michael wouldn't be left with the bill. I rang the treatment centre and explained that May was the anniversary of the accident and Michael was starting to deteriorate. I said that I hoped they would be able to start the treatment in June and they agreed to, which was a positive.

Michael had spoken to me about why he'd started smoking cannabis. It broke my heart when he said it was the only thing that helped him sleep and stopped the night terrors. The sleeping tablets made him like a zombie during the day, and he wanted to be normal during the day - well as normal as he could be.

Universal Credit contacted me again to inform me that they were not back paying him. I told them I would not appeal, as it had been a nightmare from the beginning. I also told them, that me explaining to every Tom, Dick and Harry about Michael's health over and over again was sending me crazy. In fact I changed the name of Universal Credit to Universal Shitit. There was no escape from the fact that the different departments should share the information – but they obviously didn't!

I was Michael's appointee and it was getting me that stressed that I asked who else could be the appointee? They advised me that there was a charity that could be an appointee and I thought that might actually be an option if things didn't settle down, as I needed to recover.

I couldn't wait for Michael's treatment to start as I might 'get him back' a bit more. And Universal Shitit, could stick their benefits right up their arse where the sun didn't shine…

May 17th 2019 was my grandson Elliot's first birthday. I couldn't believe another year had passed. He's really big for his age and he's definitely a 'daddy's boy'. He'd brought so much light into my life and he'd also helped Michael, who absolutely adores him.

Elliot's birthday party went really well. The kids all had a lovely time, the adults were all laughing and Michael was telling me how bad-tempered Elliot could be. He showed me what Elliot did when he was trying to move something but it wouldn't move. It was lovely to see Michael enthusiastic and laughing. And I couldn't help but wish that he was like it more often. I actually felt peace for that moment and then again when I thought that the 25th would pass without him realising...

THE RIPPLE EFFECT

I got back in the car, put the radio on and heard that Offsted had rated the local social services as inadequate. I couldn't help but think that was generous. Even though I love fostering, it's one of the best things I've done, but I've seen it first-hand how the social workers let the kids down. I'm not the only foster carer who has seen it, there must be thousands of us. You have to blame the government as they have huge workloads and not enough social workers. It's the same as the NHS - overworked, underpaid with not enough staff and bursting at the seams. The government has a lot to answer for.

And who would have thought in 2019 that we would need foodbanks just so that the less fortunate can eat, and that the elderly would be scared to put on their heating?

Ex-servicemen and women are homeless with no help and are having to beg - and there's definitely not enough help for the mentally ill. But I do believe in karma, so when I die my soul will move to a better place, and those fat, greedy, selfish politicians' souls will go to where it's hot and the sun doesn't shine...

CHAPTER 22
STILL NO CLOSURE...

On May 20th I was hit by another bombshell. I found out that Michael had spent £100s and sold some of his stuff to buy more cannabis.

I can 100% say that he was now definitely addicted and he depended on it just to feel normal. He would end up losing his little family. So not only had he got PTSD, but he was now also addicted to cannabis. I know some people will say cannabis is nothing to worry about, but it is when you think you need it just to be normal. It hadn't helped that one of Michael's friends, Simon, had showed his ugly head and had become a bad influence on him as far as I was concerned. Simon hadn't had a good childhood and smoked cannabis all the time. I actually blamed him quite a bit as he was the one who introduced Michael to it and got him on it in the beginning. I know people might say that Michael had his own mind but he hadn't - PTSD has it. Michael told me that he knew Simon from school but I didn't remember him. He also said that after the accident Simon was his only friend, but to me he was Michael's drug feeder!

I felt like grabbing Michael and saying to him, "Are you going to lose everything for cannabis?"

His dad thought it was best not to say anything, as

Michael only became verbally aggressive with me if I did. A thought flew through my mind though - thanks again Owen for taking my son's life so bad that I don't even recognise him. I needed to stop blaming Owen and Michael needed to take responsibility for his own actions.

I'd always be there for Elliot and the girls and supported Larissa with whatever she wanted to do. Even though we didn't always see eye to eye, she is an amazing mum. I also had my foster children to care for, so Michael needed to decide - family or drugs? He couldn't have both!

I wished Simon would just crawl away. I know people might think I was always blaming everyone else but that was how I felt, as Michael used to be well and he loved life but now I'd lost him as the rollercoaster started up again. And if anyone who reads my story could help me to make him well and show him that he doesn't need cannabis, I'd be forever grateful. Because I just don't know what to do anymore.

The next time I spoke to Larissa I found out that things were a lot worse than I thought. Michael was on a '£10 a day' habit. He did it to feel normal. Even though he didn't do it in front of the kids he shouldn't be doing it at all. And to me he was smoking cannabis instead of taking his medication. There was no chance that Larissa was going to let him move in until he gave up cannabis. I'd been paying for his medication every month and he'd not even been taking it. He said that the medication made him feel empty whereas cannabis made him feel normal.

He was starting to spiral out of control and we were

going to get the full force of PTSD. Could someone out there please help me make him better? He needed to be put in rehabilitation and put back on the right medication. We had to send him to America and make him stay for as long as it took. But all I could do was to ensure his bills were paid. From that one stupid day, a young man had lost his life and another lost his mind.

There was me thinking everything was moving smoothly but it wasn't! He'd been deteriorating for the last eight weeks.

The next day I went to the MP Karl Turner's office to tell him how bad Universal Credit is and to see if he could help. But the office was shut and you can only book appointments by ringing up! But someone really needs to help with this Universal shit, because it's beyond a joke. Nearly three months had gone by and they were still asking me the same bloody questions. No wonder my blood pressure gets dangerously high.

On May 23rd I had a text reminder that Michael's health assessment was due the following week. So I rang them and explained everything to them again and they advised me that they hadn't received the 113 form. I explained to them that they must have received it as the manager from the doctor's surgery had told me on the phone that she was faxing it to them.

The man said to leave it with him and he would call me back. The whole system is well and truly fucked! No one knows anything and nothing gets passed on. I just hoped they found it by the following day.

Fantastic! The man kept his promise and he rang me the next day to say they had found it and it was in hand.

THE RIPPLE EFFECT

I was still finding myself being angry with Owen as Michael deteriorated again in front of my eyes. I should have been ashamed of myself as Owen did pay the ultimate price. I really needed a fairy godmother to help me to fix him and help him to love life again and build up his self-esteem. I was even willing to kiss a donkey's arse if anybody was willing to help. I would do anything to help to get my boy back. If anyone has children who they love, I'm sure they'd be the same if they had a lost boy.

Then - OMG - I couldn't believe it - he hadn't been paid by Asda again! It was the second month that he hadn't been paid. I would have to chase them again. Why didn't anything ever run smoothly?

I spoke to somebody and they said they'd ring me back. I really felt like I was past caring.

No compensation. No wages. The only thing that ran smoothly was PIP - and the worst thing ever was the Universal shit! I couldn't believe that it was five years on and nothing much had changed.

Michael said that as soon as he wakes up - and even though he tries to bury him from his thoughts - the first thing that he thinks about is Owen. Larissa said Michael still shouts and cries in his sleep and after a night like that the sadness normally stays with him for the next few days. The darkness must stick to him like glue. I treasure the good days when I see the love between him and his little boy.

I asked myself this question once before - Can you ever be truly free from the parasite PTSD? If you know that it is possible, please find me and give me hope…

The next time I saw Michael he had tears running down his face and he just said, "I want to be normal, I want to feel happy."

I always say the same thing, "Cannabis won't help," and his reply is always that the tablets do nothing for him. Again your damned if you do and damned if you don't.

He says his night terrors are different if he hasn't had any cannabis. He says that he dreams that Owen's mum is chasing him and she is trying to take Elliot.

I told him that when he starts his new treatment he needs to tell them all this and he needs to go back to the doctors and get put back on some other medication. He then asked if we could stop talking about it and we changed the subject.

We began talking about Elliot and how he always runs with his arms in the air to kiss his daddy. I kissed him and told him that I loved him. But for me I felt broken again. The tears that no one sees filled my eyes because I will always make sure that the ripple effect stops at me…

May 25th 2019 was the fifth anniversary of the day when our world was turned upside down and our hell on earth began. On that day I went to Owen's grave again to leave some more flowers and to speak to him.

I said to him, "If there's a heaven and if you can hear me Owen, I'm sorry for being angry with you again. Please rescue Michael and show him the way and help him to be happy again."

I never told Michael I had been, as I didn't talk about anything with him to do with that day...

THE RIPPLE EFFECT

It's now more than five years since the accident and Michael is still broken.

There's still no ending. There's still no closure.

Michael is still mentally tortured and he still suffers from anxiety and stress.

Will he ever be truly happy again?

As for me, I still plod along looking after my family and still fight to help Michael to recover from PTSD. This will continue for as long as that takes and I will live with the ripple…

Sue Jorgensen, 2019